Pentecostal Preaching

Charles T. Crabtree

Gospel Publishing House
Springfield, Missouri
02-0850

Contents

ACKNOWLEDGMENTS

As I write this book, I am serving in the position of assistant general superintendent of the Assemblies of God. Although passionate about being part of this great Fellowship, I, along with our general superintendent, Thomas E. Trask, believe the Assemblies of God is just a part of the greater body of Christ and a significant member of the worldwide Pentecostal Church. In other words, I write this book as a member of the Pentecostal church, not as an executive in a Pentecostal organization. It is my desire that all ministers be comfortable in reading, teaching, or preaching from this volume. That is the reason why the Assemblies of God is not mentioned except in a couple of anecdotal references.

At places in the book, I have used the masculine pronoun as a way of avoiding awkwardness and redundancy, not because I am unaware of the contribution of women to the Pentecostal church. My mother was a powerful Pentecostal preacher/teacher, so I came by my admiration of women preachers early and naturally. But in spite of the fact the Pentecostal church has a multitude of women preachers, for which I am grateful, the majority of ordained preachers are men.

I would be remiss if I did not express deep appreciation for my editor, Glen Ellard, and my executive administrative assistant and technical editor, Jackie Chrisner. They were an immeasurable help in making this book more accurate and readable.

Note that the following abbreviations have been used in the text:

JB: Jerusalem Bible
Phillips: *The New Testament in Modern English*
RSV: Revised Standard Version
TEV: Today's English Version
TLB: *The Living Bible*
Williams: *The New Testament in the Language of the People*

Introduction

There are several reasons I was compelled to write a book on Pentecostal preaching, but I would be hard pressed to place them on a scale of importance. With that disclaimer, I will attempt a logical explanation for another volume on preaching and give some rationale for its structure and style.

DEFINING MY TERMS

For almost one hundred years, there was very little confusion about the distinctiveness of Pentecostal preaching. However, by the turn of the twenty-first century, the term "Pentecostal" was being debated and questioned, not only by evangelicals but also by Pentecostals/Charismatics. Obviously, if there is a lack of clarity in defining the meaning of Pentecostal, the integrity and distinctiveness of Pentecostal preaching will be greatly diminished.

For over 50 years I have lived and preached as a Pentecostal. There has never been any ambiguity in my mind about what it means to be Pentecostal. I am not a "classical Pentecostal," a "neo-Pentecostal," or a "Charismatic Pentecostal." I truly believe I am a "biblical Pentecostal." That may sound arrogant and boastful, but it reflects my belief that when we move away from biblical roots and definitions, we doom ourselves to endless debate with nonproductive results.

I became a Pentecostal when I received the same gift the New Testament believers received, namely, the gift of the Holy Spirit with the initial physical evidence of speaking with other tongues. That experience opened the door for me to live the Spirit-filled life as a Pentecostal believer and to minister as a Pentecostal preacher. It has been my joy almost every day of my adult life to pray with my understanding as well as in my prayer language. It has been my privilege to operate in spiritual gifts. None of this happened because I have unusual human abilities or am superior to non-Pentecostals. It is because I believe I am nothing but a channel or a resource God has chosen to flow through when I have had sense enough to surrender my will and preconceptions to Him.

It is my deep conviction the American pulpit must stop ministering questions and begin to minister Jesus Christ in Pentecostal power. The preacher of this generation who sets a goal to please people will please few, but those who have a passionate desire to please God and do His will and works will not only please God but also bless many. It is time to stop questioning the validity of speaking in tongues and begin a quest to realize every divine promise and receive every spiritual gift for the purpose of introducing the living Christ to every unbelieving American.

Why wouldn't every God-ordained preacher want to preach the centrality and preeminence of Christ with such an anointing that the most depraved, deceived, and cynical unbeliever would be convicted of sin, convinced of Christ's righteousness as Savior and Lord, and awakened to God's wrath and judgment? That is exactly what the Holy Spirit will do, not to condemn people but to make it possible for them to have a redemptive confrontation with the Son of God.

Are there any sincere preachers in America who would not want miracles of healing and other signs and wonders to follow their preaching of the Word of God? To have a significant, spiritual impact upon this nation and culture, all that and more will be needed.

Therefore, this book seeks to raise the awareness of the divine potential in and through a Pentecostal ministry and pulpit. If that goal is accomplished, I am confident there will be no confusion about defining the word "Pentecostal." Instead, there will be rejoicing at the return of an unquestionably biblical Pentecost in preaching and practice.

RESISTING THE NEGLECT OF PREPARATION

One of the constant struggles the Pentecostal preacher of today must contend with is the temptation to neglect preparation of the heart or the mind—and in some instances both.

Everybody wants to win, it has been said. But the difference between those who win and those who lose is determined by those who prepare to win and those who do not. The pulpit has the pitfall of allowing preachers the option of not preparing to win, of neglecting concentrated preaching preparation. The temptation is to make "helps" their primary source for sermon material. Young preachers need to understand they must become their own taskmasters. No one is going to make them into diligent students and hardworking ministers. Unless discipline is part of their ministry, both they and their constituency will suffer spiritual loss. All too often, men and women ordained by God fall into a pattern of mediocrity fueled by apathy. If they are not alert, they will end up maintaining that record throughout their lives.

The Pentecostal preacher lives in double jeopardy of falling into a pattern of neglect for pulpit preparation. Besides the sermonic material at hand—in books, on tape, on the Web, and in monthly and even weekly publications—is the temptation to presume on "the anointing" as a fallback for laziness.

This book does not present a quick fix for those aspiring to be Pentecostal preachers. To the contrary, I have sought to present the pulpit ministry as one of the most difficult, complex, demanding, and unrelenting responsibilities in the world. My target audience is those men and women who have a great desire to become more effective as Pentecostal preachers and are willing to pay the price. (Reading a book about the ministry would go against the grain of that other kind of preacher.)

I feel sorry for those who do not seek to excel in their pulpit ministries. They don't know what they're missing. They seldom experience the joy of having the Spirit of God drop a seed thought in their hearts and seeing that seed develop into an effective message through prayer and concentrated thinking. They will never develop their potential. Don't they realize they are cheating themselves as well as those who listen! Add to this the fact they themselves are going to have to listen to every sermon they will ever preach. (This alone should be enough to make the indolent think twice.)

This is a wonderful time in church history to be a dedicated Pentecostal preacher. Centuries of great preaching are available in many forms. The ease of travel and high-tech communication make it possible to interface with great contemporary religious thinkers and visit role model churches. This is a day of unprecedented networking. The most isolated pastor in the most remote place has an incredible wealth of resources available. As never before, Pentecostal preachers have the privilege of furthering their formal education, and in most cases, they should.

However, an abundance of resources carries the same danger as great wealth. Rather than remaining a means to enrich the soul and build the kingdom of God, both have a tendency to become ends in themselves. And what shall it profit preachers if they gain a world of religious thought and lose the soul of their ministries? So at the risk of being labeled anti-education, I have urged great caution to those who pursue education's benefits.

The ethos of education is the intellect. The ethos of Pentecost is the supernatural. The danger in exercising both is pride in human achievement. In the early days of the twentieth century, Pentecostal leaders, on the whole, were out of balance in their warnings about the misuse of education. Today the Pentecostal world is out of balance in its concern and warnings about the misuse of the supernatural. Pentecostals must be aware of the danger and potential in both arenas. Therefore, in this book, I attempt to address the potential abuse of both.

Pentecostal educators have a grave responsibility to inspire a new generation of preachers to acquire the finest education but in a way that motivates them, like the Apostle Paul, to lay their diplomas and degrees at the feet of Jesus, knowing that without His blessing, enablement, and anointing, all human gifted-ness and acquired skills are worthless.

American audiences are becoming more and more educated. Consequently, the Pentecostal preacher must give attention to—through educational disciplines—personal barriers such as an inadequate systematic theological foundation, poor grammar, racial insensitivity, or disastrous people skills. The highly educated, Spirit-filled preacher can be effective with more audiences than the poorly educated, Spirit-filled preacher. Pentecostal preachers need to know the Spirit of God is not grieved by higher education but by pride, whether in an advanced degree or in self-righteous ignorance.

The role of higher education for Pentecostal preaching is clear. Let the preachers do all they can do to "strive for masteries" (2 Timothy 2:5, KJV) so the Master himself can do all He wants to do through them.

NO SUBSTITUTE FOR THE PULPIT

At the time of the writing of this book, the role of preaching itself has diminished in many American churches. Sadly, some Pentecostal churches have decided to become "more relevant to the culture" at the cost of less time for the pulpit. I have a fervent prayer for every ordained preacher of the gospel: To realize the only way to more effectively reach the lost and establish believers in a spiritually resistant culture is by becoming a better preacher/teacher with a fresh anointing.

The pastor who substitutes anything that takes away from the pulpit is making a grave mistake. To diminish the role of preaching, especially Pentecostal preaching, is to question God's wisdom. The preaching and teaching of the Word has been and will be a divine priority until Jesus comes. That is not to say there is not a myriad of preaching styles, such as the use of drama and technology. In the end, however, no true church can survive as part of the body of Christ without a divinely appointed minister consistently declaring the gospel.

It is interesting and at the same time sad to hear the various excuses used to justify less time for pulpit ministry. Everything pastors say they want to accomplish, such as "creating more worshippers" or "appealing to and reaching youth," can be better accomplished through a more effective pulpit.

The Pentecostal church must maintain the centrality of the pulpit. All the drama, giving, programs, singing, and "preliminaries" must support and lead to a more effective pulpit.

OPEN TO THE SPONTANEITY OF THE SPIRIT

One of the hallmarks of Pentecost has been the Spirit's spontaneity that often changes the order of a service without notice. Time after time God has broken through well-laid plans to do "His thing" instead of "our thing." Many people are in heaven today because a Pentecostal preacher felt the impulse to stop in the middle of a prepared sermon and give an altar appeal or call for the elders of the church to anoint the sick with oil.

The spontaneity of the Spirit is not limited just to the pulpit. Pentecostal worship has always had a supernatural flow and undergirding. When the Spirit of God orchestrates worship, an edification results which no amount of human ability can generate or duplicate. The ability to flow with the Spirit is a critical requirement for all Pentecostal ministry.

One minister of music recently complained he had become so focused on the script for worship (that which has been rehearsed and practiced) he could not change a song spontaneously because it would confuse the worship team. Clearly, performance had become more important than the anointing. The comeback to this dilemma is: "Don't you think God knows ahead of time what He wants, and if people are led of the Spirit, they can be just as anointed in practice as they are in performance?"

Pity the poor worship leader, preacher, and teacher who believe that through careful preparation they can anticipate everything God can and will do. Pity the poor church attendee who can pretty well determine what God can do in a particular service by carefully following the bulletin. Pity anyone who believes the command to do everything "in a fitting and orderly way" (1 Corinthians 14:40) is limited to human order. May all Pentecostal pulpits and worshippers maintain an anticipation of and openness to the sovereignty of the Holy Spirit and be prepared to be amazed at what God can do through human instrumentality.

ON BEING "PREACHY"

A Pentecostal preacher has written this book. In light of this fact, the reader should not be surprised to discover that its organization follows somewhat of a preaching paradigm and sermonic format. I am amused by preachers who introduce their book by apologizing for not writing like an academician or by seeking to assure the reader of having taken pains not to be preachy, as if that would be a very bad thing.

It is my prayer this book—from a Pentecostal preacher who believes preaching is the ultimate method of communicating divine truth—can be used of God as an effective message for preachers. Furthermore, I would be most pleased if any of it, in part or in whole, is "preachy" enough for the Holy Spirit to use in the pulpit through any of my colleagues.

Chapter 1

The American Pulpit

Any biblically oriented person who decided to take on the task of making a moral and spiritual assessment of America at the turn of the twenty-first century would need to be prepared for deep disappointment and heartbreak. Moral relativism has emerged as America's mainstream philosophy, allowing every false religion, pagan god, and school of atheism to become a growing influence. The Christian faith is tolerated—but only if it is not brought to bear upon the state, the courts, or the culture.

The obvious results of a wholesale dismissal of God's love and law are always the same: Human life becomes less sacred than animal life. The value of a person is judged by a checkbook, not character. The breakup of the family is expected and often applauded. A degenerate, perverted lifestyle is celebrated in the streets.

Who is to blame for the triumph of evil in a once Christian culture? And in a nonjudgmental, tolerant society, dare anyone point a finger of judgment? Nevertheless, the answer is clear. Someone must discover the fount of poison and prescribe a cure; otherwise, the life of a nation is endangered.

The answer to a sick world is neither complicated nor mysterious. From the dawn of the human race to this moment, the Creator has ordained a small segment of society to be responsible for the spiritual and moral purity of any defined group. When the God-ordained pulpit has been true to the God-given Word—both in speech and in action—the souls of peoples and nations have been redeemed and blessed. But when the voice of the prophet is silenced or the priesthood corrupted or the pulpit profaned, the tally is eternal loss and horror. Even the secular world senses this.

It is time for our nation to return to its faith, not only in God Himself but also in His choices of personnel and processes. The time has come for the ordained of God to rise up in spiritual power and set a nation free from slavery to sin. Like Moses, many have tried to deliver through their own skill and strength only to find themselves in a desert of defeat. Like Moses, many recognize the supernatural dimension of God's call. Like Moses, they thrill to the divine promise: "I have seen the bondage of my people in America and have come down to deliver!" and then, like Moses, they stand frozen in doubt and fear when God reveals His plan to bring deliverance through them.

We know Satan undermines God's authority in any venue; so we should not be surprised that next to undermining Holy Scripture, he undermines those ordained to proclaim it. His strategy is to question that very ordination, that divine right and obligation to proclaim the gospel.

Authority

The preacher who is called by God has an indestructible authority. His source of strength is literally "out of this world." His authority is internal, not external. He answers to God, not men. Any pulpit that measures its effectiveness and power only by the acceptance and affirmation of its audience will ultimately fail that audience.

The history of God's dealings with His people and the Church as an institution can be told to a great extent by measuring the influence of externalization against the influence of divine absolutes. God's ancient people always got in trouble when they sought the affirmation of pagan neighbors instead of divine approval. The triumph of Christendom at the peak of

Charlemagne's reign was no triumph after all. It was a trade-off. The popular was substituted for the pure. Christianity was adulterated.

The revival of true religion is always a response to the misuse of externalism. Martin Luther found faith apart from the wealth, liturgy, and ecclesiastical order of the church. John Wesley was used of God to set aside a dead formalism for a quickening of spiritual life within the common people. The authority of the pulpit was restored by an internal recognition through the Spirit. The principle at work in this process must always be clear. Ultimate loyalty must be to the living God, not to a tradition kept alive through an external program or process. "The letter kills [even the most beautifully structured and appealing], but the Spirit gives life" (2 Corinthians 3:6).

To a great degree, the American pulpit lacks authority because it seeks to respond primarily to external stimuli instead of to the Spirit of God. A knowledge of the external will not cure a denomination's decline nor a church's sinking attendance. A cure is administered by divine guidance and obedience to the eternal.

Maintained by Prayer

Of course, the ability to maintain a strong, internal relationship is through prayer. This fact is indisputable. Prayer is mandated by the commands of Scripture and exemplified by the earthly relationship of the Son to the Father, and it is obvious in the lives of those preachers who have made and are making a real difference for time and eternity.

The prayerless pulpit will ultimately become a godless pulpit. Too often, men's guidance in books, tapes, and current events has substituted for the Lord of the Church as the source of continuous truth. Prayer is the only medium available for the preacher to maintain his authority for speaking for God.

In addition, the authority of the prophet has always rested upon an uncompromising obedience to proclaim God's message fresh *from* an encounter with God. The

Word of the Lord is the Word of the Lord *to* a culture, never from a culture. The true preacher is not interested in fashioning a message to scratch itching ears but to quicken dead souls.

When tradition deteriorates to an authority based upon an elaborate analysis or a presentation only to please the senses, then no freshness, spontaneity, variety, or individuality remains. Christian doctrine becomes an end in itself, resulting in a theoretical Christianity isolated from life.

On the whole, the American preacher has denounced a formal orthodoxy, which appeals only to the sensual and intellectual. In this, a great error is avoided. The younger generation has exposed the folly of confusing spiritual authority with only a mental argument or a sentimental journey. They have no interest in a religious tradition void of life.

In rejecting formal orthodoxy and a tradition of ritual as a basis for ministry, however, the preacher must be very careful to examine the "why" behind the rejection. Is the preacher motivated by a conviction born of God's Spirit or simply because the culture is no longer buying tradition? If it is the latter, the preacher has moved from one kind of death to another. A corpse dressed in the latest fashion may be more attractive than the one in old clothes, but the condition of the corpse is the same.

Is the preacher's authority based solely upon the ability to read, interpret, and appeal to the contemporary lifestyle? Then he hazards the delusion he is a success because people are attracted to the church. True success can be measured only by the redemptive work of God done in transforming power through the Holy Spirit, and that power flows through open communication with heaven in prayer.

Drawn from Heaven

The authority of the preacher must forever be the same as that of Jesus Christ. He revealed His authority for ministry in John 5:

> [19]Jesus gave them this answer: I tell you the truth, the Son can do nothing by himself; he can do only what he sees his Father doing, because whatever the Father does the Son also does.
> [26]For as the Father has life in himself, so he has granted the Son to have life in himself. [27]And he has given him authority to judge because he is the Son of Man. [30]By myself I can do nothing; I judge only as I hear, and my judgment is just, for I seek not to please myself but him who sent me. [31]If I testify about myself, my testimony is not valid.

These words of Jesus, among His last on earth, should echo in the heart of every preacher in any century: "As the Father has sent me, I am sending you" (John 20:21).

If Jesus were to preach in the twenty-first century, He would proclaim the kingdom of God. His message would be eternally relevant. Without a doubt, He would amaze everyone by His lack of interest in being culturally relevant. He would undoubtedly dress in modern clothes and use modern transportation and contemporary parables to illustrate truth, but His unswerving loyalty to eternal truth would be offensive to the "religiously correct" or the most up-to-date schools of thought. However, He would begin every day in prayer. He would seek out the lost and save the sinner. He would open the Scriptures in every church in which He preached. He would be aware of the hurts and longings of the people, but He would never modify truth or doctrine to find an open door. He would offend many by identifying himself as the narrow gate, the only way to heaven. He would point to the cross and to His blood as the Lamb of God. He would not be popular as an ecumenist. He would warn of judgment to come. His "power people" (disciples in the inner circle) would be few and come primarily from the lower middle class. His strength would come from heaven and His authority from the living God, His Father. His words would astound. His works would be supernatural.

The preacher is given divine authority from heaven. He is not a creature of the state. Not being commissioned by the state, he has a freedom that those who are do not have. Society cannot create a person to be a poet; even so, it is beyond the authority of any state, however powerful, to create a prophet. Therefore, because the preacher, the messenger of God, is not the elect of the state, he is the master of society. He is not the pawn of a culture but the mouthpiece of God.

The importance of divine authority cannot be overemphasized. The ordained and anointed of God must never become enslaved in whole or in part to a culture, because they are not dependent upon it. Furthermore, no change in society can alter, let alone cancel, the commission of the preacher.

Since Satan had the audacity to tempt, with a promise of the temporal, the head of the Church to bow to his authority, it stands to reason he would systematically do the same to mere members of that Church. The world seeks to undermine preachers by tempting them to put the culture and the external first, and at times the Church itself has undermined the authority of its ordained by adopting a carnal criteria. Consequently, the God-ordained preacher of the gospel in this day must have an internal authority, which results in a security no external force can erode or destroy.

It must frustrate and confound the councils of heaven to see those ordained by God and anointed by the Spirit bound by the fear of mortals—so afraid of being out of touch with society rather than out of touch with God. Can you imagine heaven's comments when a preacher says, "I don't dare mention the cross, the blood, holiness, or hell because I'm afraid how people will respond"? With one voice heaven answers, "It is not the prerogative of any preacher to delete, distort, or determine one word of God's message."

God authorizes the preaching of His gospel and chooses whom He will to preach it—it is His prerogative. In many cases, He chooses to call those who do not fit human criteria. The dictum of Scripture that "not many mighty . . . are called" (1 Corinthians 1:26) is as applicable today as the day it was written. It is a fact some of the most effective and productive ministries throughout time have been people the world considered "uneducated and untrained" (Acts 4:13, NKJV).

The importance of continuing education for the contemporary preacher is vital to his ministry. If he wants to connect God's unchanging message to today's audience, he will seek to understand the thinking of his generation. However, continuing education determines only a measure of one's effectiveness, not divine authorization. What the preacher does with his divine ordination is a continuing responsibility between him and the One who called him. When ecclesiastical bodies use external measurements alone to determine God's ordination upon a man or a woman, they fall into the trap of equating the spiritual with the temporal. Church leadership should always insist a person make full proof of his ministry, but the proofs should be examined from the viewpoint of both the spiritual and the human.

Responsibility

When the preacher has settled his authority, he more easily determines his responsibilities. That is no small assignment in a day of rapid communication and travel. However, it is obvious there is no more or no less time in the twenty-first century than there was in the first century. In spite of this fact, many in ministerial circles insist there is now less time for prayer than twenty years ago and nowhere near the time for sermon preparation our forefathers had. They have the erroneous idea the only responsibilities and demands on preachers of bygone days were to meditate, study, and prepare sermons all day.

Set Agenda

When anyone in any field of endeavor wishes to grapple with responsibility, the temptation is to begin making excuses. Nowhere is this more pronounced than in the ministerium. More than most others, the preacher has the freedom to set his own agenda and fulfill his primary responsibilities.

In the twentieth century, the American pulpit was greatly weakened because many preachers mistook people's demands on their time as commands from God. Added to this pressure was an erosion of responsibility to be one's best in the pulpit. The pulpit took a terrible hit from its own occupants. The problem was exacerbated by self-fulfilling prophecies about the pulpit. It was said, for example, preaching is no longer a priority in the life of the church because weak and ineffective preachers have lost influence in the culture.

The ordained preacher of today has the same responsibilities as his predecessors. The first of those responsibilities, the ultimate priority, is to know and obey God's will. Christ articulated and fulfilled it: "By myself I can do nothing; I judge only as I hear, and my judgment is just, for I seek not to please myself but him who sent me" (John 5:30 NIV).

It would be ludicrous to believe it is God's will for any preacher to stride to the pulpit unprepared in spirit or mind. Yet because the preacher has had too many self-inflicted human demands on his time, many modern congregations receive nothing of substance week after week.

The leaders of the New Testament church knew of such demands, particularly when the church grew. They found themselves meeting social demands (caring for and feeding widows) and neglecting their God-ordained responsibilities. They woke up one day and in essence said, "Look, this doesn't make sense. We are called to preach. We dare not allow any human demand—as valid as it may be—to undermine God's authority and our responsibility to Him. We'll delegate this demand to Spirit-filled people and get back to prayer and study of the Word."

The pulpit may not be as important as it was to many, but "many" should not determine the value of, and attendant responsibility to, anything God has ordained. If ministers across the board responded to the demands of people in the same way as the apostles, the whole contemporary church would undoubtedly be pleased! The result would be a dynamic, growing church.

Every person ordained of God to the preaching ministry has enough time to always be at his best in the pulpit. God has never authorized and assigned someone to a task knowing that person could not fulfill that responsibility according to His will.

Serve One Master

Jesus' warning about serving two masters is never more significant than when applied to the ministry. When ministers do not fulfill responsibilities to the ruling authority, they will—by default—choose another authority. However, there comes an ironic reckoning: In choosing to please others rather than God, they ultimately lose their authority with them. They become double losers: (1) of the divine authority from God and (2) of the respect of those they have chosen to please.

If, on the other hand, the preacher truly obeys God and puts His kingdom first, he is a double winner. He pleases God and in doing so pleases the members of His kingdom. Truly mature Christians want their minister to put God first in his own life and ministry. It is the carnal Christian who, by definition, is a selfish person, always making demands on the preacher even if it means compromising the preacher's responsibility to God and the church.

The spiritually strong, spiritually effective pastor accepts the God-given responsibility for his pulpit, starting with himself. There is no great mystery or complicated process to fulfilling that responsibility. Ninety percent of being a good preacher is being a good Christian—a disciplined follower of Christ.

One popular minister said he did not need to pray that much because so many people were praying for him. What utter nonsense! God is not about to tell others what He wants to tell the preacher. No one else can be responsible for another's spiritual condition. Many would love to hire someone to go to the gym every morning and do a workout for them with the same results as if they had done it themselves.

Only responsible people should fill responsible positions. There is no more responsible assignment on earth greater than being a servant of God and a voice for God. The only way to fulfill that responsibility is to be responsible to Him.

Paul the Apostle addressed the distinct possibility that even he, after receiving his divine ordination and responding to it, could become a castaway. How does this happen? By irresponsibility in word and/or deed. All of us have been saddened to see those who were obviously qualified for great ministries be disqualified for a few moments of sinful pleasure.

May the expectations for an evangelical/Pentecostal preacher always meet heaven's expectations. If the day ever comes in America that the behavior of a man of God is no higher than a man of sin, the subsequent spiritual calamity would be incalculable. To a great extent, the medium is the message. "The Word was made flesh, and dwelt among us" (John 1:14). That is the reason God did not choose angels to be His preachers. The Word as lived out through human flesh moved from the theoretical to the practical in purity.

The last half of the past century saw an intensification of immorality in America which rivaled the final days of the Roman empire. The culture became saturated with sex to the point of unbridled license. The pulpit survived because the leaders of the Pentecostal Church were spiritual enough to make its ministers accountable to God. May no less be said for the twenty-first-century Church.

Focus on the Pulpit

One of the greatest threats to the pulpit is negligence in pulpit preparation. Someone has well said, "The preacher must be his own Simon Legree and Pharaoh." Maintaining a diligence and focus in sermon preparation can be a real struggle at times. The trouble begins when a preacher is applauded for a great message when he knows he "got by" without much prayer or study. In a very short time, the pattern of "getting by" becomes habitual and the expectation of the congregation is lowered to mediocrity.

One of the greatest challenges facing the twenty-first-century American preacher is raising the congregation's level of expectation for the pulpit. This can be done only at the local level. It is there that God's people determine true values for real life. They expect televised ministers to be "special" or "out of the ordinary," but no Christian can mature by television alone. The pulpit in the local setting—week-by-week, face-to-face—is in a unique position to accomplish the full force of God's intention when He chose "the message of the cross" (1 Corinthians 1:18) to make an eternal difference in the lives of men and women.

The minister is accountable to God to be at his very best within the framework of his responsibility. If God had wanted him to be someone else, He would have made him someone else. If God wanted the preacher to be responsible for a TV audience, He would have given him a TV audience. The American pulpit does not rise and fall on the strength of celebrity; it rises and falls upon the dedication and devotion of those who week-by-week faithfully minister the word to all sizes of congregations.

Every local church is a divine franchise with God-ordained oversight in the person of a pastor. The effectiveness of a local "franchise" affects the reputation of the entire worldwide enterprise. The responsibility of the local church is going to become greater in the future, not less. The individual minister will become of more importance than ever before, for the care and need of eternal souls are in God's plan addressed locally, not nationally.

The contemporary preacher has great authority, and with that comes an awesome responsibility—far beyond the moment and the numbers in his visible audience. He bears a responsibility to God and will give an account of his ministry to Him. He bears a responsibility to himself and his family. The quality of his own spiritual life and that of his family will, to a large extent, be determined by the measure of his passion and preparation for the pulpit. He has a responsibility to his congregation. It is his task to hear from God and herald God's truth for the heart and soul of his congregation. He has a responsibility to his peers. When he does his best, he raises the influence of all pulpits in the minds of the hearers.

The modern-day pulpit tempts its occupant to become frustrated and lose hope. However, when the preacher has a security in his divine call and realizes he ultimately must please only one master—not many—the responsibility becomes a glorious task, because he lives by heaven's expectation through a divine enablement.

There is a wonderful paradox in being obedient to God above all others. When we are weak, then are we strong. When we seek to please God, we please people as well.

In a day when the pulpit is viewed as a third-level task, the American preacher must make some very hard choices in setting priorities. The twenty-first-century preacher has the same level of responsibility to God and the pulpit as did his predecessors. He does not have the time nor the ability to do all that he wants to do—certainly not all that others want him to do—but he does have the time to do all God expects Him to do.

Destiny

We have acknowledged the authority and responsibility of the pulpit. It is now necessary to address the destiny of the American pulpit in the twenty-first century. The classic story of the mean little boy who held a small bird in his fist and asked "Will this bird live or die?" is applicable. The answer of the wise man for the life of the bird is the same for the life of the pulpit: "It is in your hands." It is within the power of the one who has the responsibility of the pulpit. Saying that, there is a divine destiny which will never allow the pulpit to remain empty and the Church devoid of God's message.

Regardless of how evil the culture or how many ineffective preachers fill the pulpits, there will always be a place (temporal trials as well as eternal rewards included) for the true prophet of God. As much as Satan and all his followers may scheme and attack, the pulpit is not going away. God is going to keep on ordaining His messengers.

Should the Lord tarry, those who live out their ministries within the United States in the twenty-first-century have the promise of the most exciting, challenging, dangerous, complex, and rewarding opportunities in history.

The challenges are obvious. From within, the church will struggle to maintain a pure gospel and absolute truth while warding off godless lifestyles. From without, the challenges will include intrusive laws that could result in faithful ministers being jailed for standing against biblically identifiable sin. The preaching of holiness will be targeted as a hate crime by the unrighteous. City ordinances will seek to control ministries through building codes. Financial benefits such as tax deductions for churches will come under hostile scrutiny with an almost certain negative outcome.

"When the enemy shall come in like a flood, the Spirit of the Lord shall lift up a standard against him" (Isaiah 59:19). The more overwhelming the antichurch movement becomes, the greater the need for God-ordained ministers to call their towns and cities to repentance. The coming persecution of the Church will not defeat the true Church; it will simply purify it. A Chinese Christian, speaking at a ministerial confer-ence, has made a statement the American church should take to heart: "We have very little problem with hypocrisy in the Chinese Christian church."

If I had a child ordained by God to be a preacher in the year 2010, I would have all the natural, human fears of an anxious father; but as a preacher-father, I would be excited and thrilled. I know God-called preachers will never be without a message for their generation; thus, they will always have a place to proclaim that message.

This nation is crying for an army of powerful preachers to invade her cities and towns. But such an invasion must come with a divine authority, a love for God, and a message of truth. Our communities need light for the darkness, fullness of the Spirit for the emptiness of materialism, living water for parched souls, and the bread of life to strengthen the famished. The twenty-first-century pulpit awaits the coming of the prophet.

Chapter 2

The Pentecostal Pulpit

Is there any difference between a preacher who has received the baptism in the Holy Spirit with the evidence of tongues and one who has not?

There certainly should be. If there is no difference, why was Jesus adamant in His command to His disciples they must not preach and minister without receiving this experience? If there is no difference, why is there so much instruction in the Scriptures concerning tongues and other supernatural gifts? These directives were given to ministers to help them instruct people about the purpose and use of the gifts, both publicly and privately, and to emphasize the work of the Spirit. It is inconceivable to think the Lord of the Church would command His ministers to preach and teach regarding the supernatural demonstration of the Holy Spirit and they themselves not be empowered to use these gifts. If there were no difference, why would the Apostle Paul, whom every minister seeks to emulate, openly admit, "I thank God that I speak in tongues more than all of you" (1 Corinthians 14:18).

Perhaps many reject the need for a preacher to have the Pentecostal experience because they have observed a remarkable effectiveness in some who deny the experience. And perhaps they have coupled that with observing an equally remarkable ineffectiveness in some who have believed and received. It seems a multitude of ministers have declined this wondrous dimension of spiritual life and power solely upon anecdotal evidence.

Untold numbers remain lost today because they have observed people who claim to be Christians yet show little or no difference between themselves and unbelievers. In some cases, Christians may even be viewed as hypocritical, dishonest, and mean. However, the misrepresentation of something should not determine its validity. And certainly in matters of faith, one should not turn from Scripture to human expression for a basis on which to make a definitive decision.

Seeing the Need

In spite of God's obvious blessings and sovereign ordination of many non-Pentecostal ministries, His provision remains for a solid, biblical, Christ-centered Pentecostal ministry with signs and wonders. It is not only available, in this present generation it is especially needed.

The roots of Pentecostal preaching reach back to the Twelve. Mark 3:14-15 gives insight into Jesus' calling and equipping of the disciples before Pentecost: "He appointed twelve—designating them apostles—that they might be with him and that he might send them out to preach and to have authority to drive out demons." From day one, the Lord ordained and prepared this group to take over the leadership of His Church after His ascension. He guided them, established the principles, and set the course for ministerial training. If anyone doubts the importance of good Christian higher education, that person needs to look again at the three-and-a-half-year "seminary" Jesus led for His class of twelve. It was in that school Jesus taught the great doctrines, opened spiritual understanding, and prepared His students for a supernatural ministry.

Besides being called to be preachers, the disciples were given authority and power to step into the arena of the miraculous. Jesus was preparing them for supernatural performance as well as proclamation. Later Jesus sent out seventy disciples with the same mandate. They came back and reported, with a sense of superiority and pride, great success. Surprisingly, the Lord was not impressed; He was concerned. He reminded them of how Lucifer, who had wielded unprecedented authority in the heavens, had fallen "like lightening." Christ's disciples were given power over the devil and to trample on snakes and scorpions, the symbols of Satan. Then came words of caution: "However, do not rejoice that the spirits submit to you, but rejoice that your names are written in heaven" (Luke 10:20).

Keeping Perspective

The Luke passage is most enlightening. Jesus instructed the seventy to get their eyes off what they had done through His power and focus on the greatest of all miracles, which had happened in them. Salvation must forever be the ultimate triumph of the soul, the choicest kind of harvest, and the most sought-after proof of effective preaching.

Satan's fall from heaven should be a continual warning to those who rejoice in the power of Pentecost: Do not allow spiritual gifts to become a source of pride rather than a source of enablement. The greatest preachers in the world are weak and helpless in their own strength. If the ability to perform the supernatural becomes a source of pride rather than a source of humility in a Pentecostal ministry, the preacher is in mortal danger not only of losing his ministry but also of losing his own soul. He could be rudely awakened at the final judgment. Seeking entrance to heaven because of his ability to perform miracles, he might very well hear the judge of all the earth say, in effect, "You didn't pay attention. Your pride in a miracle ministry deceived you into thinking what you did could be substituted for what I did. Miracles on earth have nothing to do with entrance into heaven." Could this be one of the reasons the Lord chose to use non-Pentecostal ministries throughout history—to humble Pentecostals and show them that the great goal of heaven is the salvation of the lost, not the performance of miracles? Sinners are saved by the miracle of Calvary, not by the gifts of the Spirit. Can anyone dispute T. L. Osborne when he exclaimed, in an Assemblies of God headquarters chapel service, "Salvation is a stupendous miracle"?

Emphasis on the Lost

The emphasis upon the lost continued in the teaching of Christ after Calvary and before Pentecost. (John 20:21-23 has been a point of unnecessary debate between Pentecostals and non-Pentecostals for many years.) The resurrected Christ declared to His disciples He was sending them forth in the same way He was sent by His Father. Then He breathed on them and said, "Receive the Holy Spirit" (v.22). When Jesus did that, the disciples received an enduement of spiritual power for effective evangelism. Jesus followed up with the purpose of this special enablement: "If you forgive anyone his sins, they are forgiven; if you do not forgive them, they are not forgiven" (v.23).

There is no question when Jesus breathed upon His disciples they received a special measure of the Spirit. This enablement prior to Pentecost by the resurrected Lord is suggestive of the work of the Spirit at salvation and in the process of discipleship apart from the gift of the Holy Spirit received in the Upper Room. The disciples were given more than the letter of the redemptive message; they were given the mandate to preach salvation in such a way the Spirit of God would speak through them with heavenly authority. They were ordained and empowered to preach the message. More than that, they were authorized to preach and identify what constituted a person's being in sin. Furthermore, as recipients of redemptive truth, they, through the Spirit, were given the glorious privilege of offering true salvation.

When Jesus gave the Holy Spirit in measure to His disciples prior to Pentecost, He was showing the vital role of the Spirit's work, whether or not a preacher was

Pentecostal in the Acts 2:4 sense. Billy Graham by testimony is not a Pentecostal who has spoken with tongues. Nevertheless, the Spirit of God has attended his preaching, drawing thousands into the Kingdom by convicting, saving, and baptizing into the body of Christ.

Prior to Pentecost, the Lord revealed to His disciples the ministry of the Spirit must be at work through anyone who is preaching to the lost. To emphasize that truth, He gave them an enduement of the Spirit. One could assume that was all the enablement needed, but such was not the case. Christ left no question about His desire the disciples He had breathed upon go to the Upper Room to receive a special enduement of power from on high. They could have easily said, "Look, we've already received the Holy Spirit. We have been authorized to preach the gospel and even tread on serpents. We are not going to wait upon God for something beyond what we already possess." But they did not. For that matter, no preacher should be satisfied with anything less than what God has promised.

A Continuing Command

Jesus commanded His disciples to wait until the Day of Pentecost before they started their public ministry. He wanted every one of them to receive the power and special authenticity they would need in His physical absence. That command was not just for 12 but for 120. If only 12 had received the gift of the Holy Spirit on the Day of Pentecost, the argument the baptism of the Spirit with the evidence of tongues had been for the 12 original apostles alone would have some validity. However, such was not the case. Jesus was launching more than a contemporary first-century church. It would be a Church for the ages. He was giving direction and revealing His will about how He wanted the Church to operate until His return. The head of the Church not only gave the Great Commission, but He also revealed the preferred modus operandi. In order for His preachers to meet the demands heaven placed upon them, Jesus knew they would need a gift of divine power in order to raise up a Spirit-empowered Church.

It is for historians to study and speculate on why the command for all believers to receive the gift of the Holy Spirit with the physical evidence of tongues began to be ignored and why the Pentecostal Church became almost nonexistent for hundreds of years. However, the preacher is not responsible for the Church and pulpit of yesteryear; he is responsible to God for the ministry and pulpit of today.

Acknowledging the Need of Help

Those ordained to fill a twenty-first-century American pulpit who are not overcome by a sense of total helplessness are a danger to the church. They are a danger because they think they are the answer to church growth and development. They are a danger because they will become comfortable with a form of religion and deny the supernatural. They are a danger because they think thoughtful sermons and good hermeneutics alone will transform lives. They are a danger because the pulpit is used for their own agendas, not for the will and Word of God.

The deplorable spiritual condition of America itself should cause every preacher within its borders to fall to their knees and cry out to God: "Without you, I can do nothing that will last, nothing that will make a significant difference in the people of my community. Lord, I need your help." Through the mercies of God, He offers such a minister of the gospel all that is needed to have an effective and powerful ministry: the promise of the Holy Spirit.

Let us suppose a young minister in his first church is offered a gift—not a material gift but the gift of a wonderful, Spirit-filled minister of advanced age with an outstanding record of building great church bodies. This man offers to come alongside the young minister at no financial cost. Furthermore, he promises to serve only at the minister's will and do nothing but support him. To a great degree, that is what Jesus has offered to every one of His ministers. The only difference is that the Person of the Holy Spirit is far superior to any aged minister, being all-wise and all-powerful without age or limitation.

It is hard to imagine any minister alive today who is not desperate for help from God. Yet, so many miss out on the priceless gift and continuing presence of the Holy Spirit's fullness because they have received false teaching about Him or perceived a misuse by those claiming to have received Him.

Instead of approaching the subject of Pentecost from a human viewpoint, the minister would find great benefit in approaching Pentecost as a divine promise. It is incumbent upon everyone in ministry to ask the question: "Is a Pentecostal pulpit going to be the most effective pulpit in the twenty-first century?" Let us answer this question with an open heart and mind, asking for the guidance of the Holy Spirit.

Revealing Christ

With divine authority, the Pentecostal pulpit will reveal Jesus Christ as He is, through the power of the Spirit resulting in living revelation and truth. If no one can say with authority "Jesus is Lord" except through the revelation of the Spirit, how dependent the preacher must become upon the Holy Spirit to bring Jesus to life in word and deed.

As the Pentecostal preacher preaches, he can antici-pate the work of the Spirit in divine conviction. Pentecostal churches around the world are filled with those who, with Paul the Apostle, confess they were the "worst of sinners" (see 1 Timothy 1:15). These people testify they were brought to a saving knowledge of Christ not by an eloquent sermon but by a deep conviction of sin and a certain knowledge that the claims of Jesus Christ as Savior and Lord are real.

Most religious leaders accept the premise America should be identified as a post-Christian and post-modern nation. The mantra of moral relativism can be expressed simply as "my truth is my truth; your truth is your truth. It is arrogant of you to tell me your truth is superior to my truth." How in the world can a preacher possibly prove anything to anyone with such a mindset? The answer is through the ministry of the Holy Spirit. For the preacher to present Christ as the "the way and the truth and the life" (John 14:6), he must have an authority beyond reason.

Fortunately, in relationship to truth the gift of the Holy Spirit is called the Comforter. In light of the terrible deception of the last days, this point cannot be overemphasized. "When the Comforter is come, whom I will send unto you from the Father, even the Spirit of truth, which proceedeth from the Father, he shall testify of me" (John 15:26, KJV). What a promise! What a comfort! What an authority!

While on earth, the Lord Jesus was the covering for His disciples. Each one could say as they looked at Jesus, "It gives us great comfort to know He is with us, telling us what to do. We would be lost without Him. If we lose Him, we will be like orphans." If the disciples felt that way—having had the privilege of sitting under the Lord's instruction, seeing Him minister in the flesh, and being guided through storms both literal and figurative—how much more those who minister twenty centuries later need such a "Comforter," such a guide and covering. The promise given to the disciples that the Lord would not leave them or forsake them holds true today. It should comfort all Pentecostal preachers to know that from the moment a new day begins until it fades into night, they are not alone in ministry. From the first thought of a message through to its delivery, the Spirit-filled minister has the source of truth and power guiding both thought and presentation.

Pentecostals have often been criticized for emphasizing the Spirit and speaking with tongues more than the person and work of Christ. Let the record be clear: A true Pentecostal will always give Jesus preeminence. He is the central message, first and last. The only reason the Holy Spirit baptism should be emphasized is to emphasize Jesus Christ and Him crucified.

The Azusa Street revival of 1906–1909 is known around the world as the visitation which thrust the Pentecostal Church into prominence. Of course, there were human elements and responses that were not of God, but the power manifested at Azusa Street brought a new awareness of Christ and a desire to go into all the world and make Him known. William J. Seymour, the pastor, would often hide behind the pulpit (a "converted" orange crate) in prayer. In the midst of great emotion, healing of the sick, and speaking in tongues, Seymour would stand behind his pulpit and emphasize over and over to the effect: "You need Jesus above all else. You need the healer more than healing, the baptizer more than the baptism."

A Pentecostal pulpit will operate under the guidance and power of the Holy Spirit; and since the Holy Spirit has come to testify of Christ, those who sit before the pulpit can expect an authoritative word from the Lord and a quickening of the Spirit. The role of the Holy Spirit is to make Jesus more real than ever before. By revelation knowledge through the Spirit, the believer is able to say, "I know Jesus Christ in living truth. The world has its truth, but I have met the Way, the Truth, and the Life."

Supernatural Demonstration

The Pentecostal pulpit will not only preach the living Word of Christ based upon the written Word of God, but it will also be accompanied by the living works of Christ in supernatural demonstration.

Jesus promised the disciples the ability not only to preach His Word but also to perform mighty miracles. In the opening verse of Acts, Luke sets the tone for Pentecostal ministry: "I wrote about all that Jesus began to do and to teach." The operative word here is "began." Jesus did not teach and perform miracles as an end in themselves but as a way to show His disciples how He wanted ministry to be done. The messages and miracles of Jesus were certainly important and powerful, but their greater importance is what He put in motion. What He "began to do and to teach" was to be followed in perpetuity by those He would call.

Jesus said, "Verily, verily, I say unto you, He that believeth on me, the works that I do shall he do also; *and greater works than these shall he do*; because I go unto my Father" (John 14:12, KJV, my emphasis). How do we know this glorious promise was to be fulfilled through a Pentecostal ministry? Because Jesus told His disciples it would be better for them if He left them physically so He could come to them spiritually through the Comforter, the Holy Spirit. He said to them, "For if I go not away, the Comforter will not come" (John 16:7, KJV). The progression is clear. Jesus had to leave so the Comforter could come. They were to wait in Jerusalem until He came in the fullness God intended. Then and only then were Jesus' followers equipped to do greater works than He had done.

A few years ago, a young African living in a large city was saved and filled with the Holy Spirit. A few months afterwards, God told him to start a Pentecostal church in his village. Every Saturday after work in the city, he would walk for hours back to his village. Every Sunday morning in simple faith he would stand in the middle of the village and preach the gospel.

However, the witchdoctor of the village had forbidden any of the villagers to listen. The young preacher became weary of no audience, so he would set up stones and preach to them. Week after week he preached to stones and would then walk many hours back to the city to prepare for work on Monday morning.

One day as he was leaving his village after having preached, a voice spoke to him from the shadow of a hut. As the preacher drew near, he saw a man, who said, "I have been listening to you every Sunday. I want to know if your Jesus can heal my boy." The preacher answered immediately that yes, He could, and walked into the hut to see a crippled boy lying on a mat. The preacher placed his hand on the boy, and instantly Jesus raised him up.

In a few moments the village was in turmoil because they saw a boy who could not walk leaping and running. Today there is a great Pentecostal church in that village. Among the members is the former witchdoctor who had forbidden the villagers to listen to a Spirit-filled preacher. This is but one example of the Pentecostal legacy.

To a great extent, the American pulpit has been bathed in unbelief. Many American preachers deny the inspiration of Scriptures; many reject the gifts of the Holy Spirit. Surprisingly, even some who have experienced the baptism of the Spirit cannot seem to believe God for a continuing flow of the supernatural. It is possible to receive a gift from God by faith but not believe the gift can be activated in continuing ministry. The Scripture warns of this error when it speaks of people starting in the Spirit but continuing in the flesh (Galatians 3:3).

For too long, the modern pulpit has proclaimed what the Holy Spirit cannot do. Using human argument and carnal logic, it has excused weakness and ineffectiveness. The preacher of today must bring the supernatural back into his ministry. Having a sense of humility in himself and a bold faith in God, he must confess God can do anything He wills through human channels.

The account of Peter and John in Acts 3 sets a wonderful example of humility and power. When the lame man at the Beautiful Gate was healed, the people approached the apostles as objects of wonder. Peter deflected any consideration of them as a source of power and righteousness. Instead, he pointed out that they had performed the miracle of healing by invoking the name of Jesus.

Nowhere in Scripture can an honest student find a word or a phrase canceling the promise of this supernatural power. To the contrary, for the past one hundred years, the Pentecostal Church has recorded literally thousands of miracles.

The late C. M. Ward, the great radio evangelist for the Assemblies of God, told of a remarkable experience he had while preaching on the radio. In the middle of his message, he was seized by the Holy Spirit and said, "Sir, the answer is not jumping off a bridge; it is a saving knowledge of Jesus Christ that will save you." A few days later, Ward received a letter that explained the incident. The writer had parked on the Golden Gate Bridge in San Francisco and prepared to get out of his car and commit suicide. For some unexplained reason, he turned up the radio and to his amazement was arrested on the spot by the Word of the Lord through an obedient minister.

The testimony of miracles through Pentecostal preaching has filled many books, yet resistance to moving into the realm of the supernatural persists. Denying the miraculous has serious consequences. For one, those who suffer disease and guilt lose. For another, those who have never beheld the works of God being supernaturally manifested also lose, not knowing the wondrous joy it brings.

The Antidote to False Religion

The Pentecostal pulpit is the antidote to false religion. America has always opened her doors to people from other lands, but in the last 25 years the numbers have accelerated. The open borders have proved to be a blessing and a curse. On the one hand, many have come with an open heart, ready to respond to the offer of salvation and blessings of the Church. On the other, the enemy has come in like a flood through demonic activity. Mysticism and false spirituality are inundating millions.

Unless a greater number of American ministers are endued with the Spirit and begin to believe for supernatural power, both in and out of the pulpit, the spiritual prospects for America look bleak. As more and more Americans seek the supernatural through the occult, eastern religions, and a mystical spirituality, more and more Americans are going to be possessed by evil spirits. Even now, the works of the devil are accelerating at an alarming rate.

Satan seeks to deceive the Church into thinking nothing can be done. But what if the Early Church had felt that way? What if missionaries on dark continents had decided the supernatural was not part of contemporary ministry? Millions would have remained in the grip of paganism. The Pentecostal dimension of ministry is the only hope for overcoming the spirit of this age. The words of the LORD of hosts that it is "not by might nor by power, but by my Spirit" (Zechariah 4:6) remain as relevant today as the day they were recorded.

A Sensitivity to the Spirit's Move

The Pentecostal pulpit has a sensitivity to the moving of the Spirit and the capacity to react spontaneously to human need. Jesus modeled responding to the immediate so God could be glorified. On His way to minister, He was often interrupted. When that happened, He would simply minister to the need presented to Him. When He was speaking, demons would sometimes cry out, and Jesus would simply stop and bring deliverance.

Throughout Pentecostal history, ministries have been marked by the God-given ability to change an order of service without notice. This kind of spontaneity has proved time and again, even to unbelievers, that God was in control.

From time to time, I have experienced a sudden knowledge that God wanted to go beyond the expected. On one occasion in the pastorate, I was teaching a Bible study in the church sanctuary. About halfway through, I heard a directive from heaven to stop the teaching and call for a woman sitting in the back to come forward; God wanted to heal her. Then and there God healed the woman of Parkinson's disease and her husband of a heart condition. The ultimate result was a building of faith within the congregation and many years of effective witnessing by that couple.

Church bulletins and orders of service are fine, but

in this day of great spiritual need and warfare, the preacher should use them as guides, not rules.

The Exercise of Gifts

The Pentecostal pulpit can and should be used of God for the preaching and exercise of the gifts of the Spirit as emphasized in 1 Corinthians 12 and 14. Some would point to 1 Corinthians 13 as a reason not to allow such gifts to operate. Chapter 13 is placed in the middle of Paul's teaching on the gifts of the Spirit to emphasize the motive of divine love, to make certain the miraculous is not canceled by pride and selfishness. However, Paul's instruction in the proper use of the gifts is not to be taken as a denial of their place in the body of Christ.

If anyone should covet the gifts of the Spirit, as Paul directs, the contemporary preacher should be first in line. These gifts are the Spirit's enablements. Of course, the gifts are not limited to the Pentecostal pulpit, but they are certainly needed by every minister.

The gifts of the Spirit are given for the purpose of edifying and profiting the entire Church. What preacher in this country does not need the Spirit's word of wisdom or knowledge, beyond sermon preparation, to help the body of Christ? From time to time the preacher needs every enablement of the gifts of faith and healing and miracles. The gifts of prophecy and the discerning of spirits are especially needed today; and since tongues with interpretation are equal to prophecy, these gifts need to operate as well.

Of course, all gifts need to be subject to the oversight and judgment of spiritual leadership. Some Pentecostal preachers, afraid they might "quench the Spirit," have allowed people to misuse gifts to the point of embarrassment and reproach. Preachers have as much of a responsibility to "quench the flesh" as they do to promote the manifestations of the Spirit.

The Pentecostal preacher should never have an attitude of superiority toward those who do not believe in the baptism of the Spirit with the initial physical evidence of other tongues, but neither should he be intimidated by those who are critical of a Pentecostal pulpit. We are not going to give an account of our ministry to mortals but to God. We must obey God rather than men.

A little over a hundred years ago, God in His wisdom decided to bring back the Pentecostal pulpit. Through the intervening years, the Pentecostal Church has grown to a mighty force in number and power. Moving into the twenty-first century, the minister continues to need that unusual anointing, that revelation faith, that ministry of miracles. This is the time to emphasize Pentecostal gifts and power!

Chapter 3
The Word: The Foundation of All Preaching

Historically, the Pentecostal pulpit has never wavered on the subject of the inerrancy of Holy Scripture. However, in recent years there has been such an erosion of this doctrine in parts of the evangelical world that it is clear no one is immune from drifting. Any book on preaching must emphasize, underscore, and reaffirm the basis for all preaching—an unwavering faith and an undying commitment to the written Word of God.

The attack on inerrancy is of course motivated by Satan, but is first articulated through academia. By its nature, it is an exercise in scholarship; and because of this fact, Pentecostals who are not highly educated are often overwhelmed by a feeling of inferiority in defending this eternal truth. Such a feeling has its roots in the past. Honesty compels Pentecostals to acknowledge the strong bias against higher education that existed in the first half of the twentieth century. The fathers of the modern Pentecostal movement voiced the inherent dangers formal education brought into the Spirit-filled church but failed to appreciate its blessings and benefits. The majority of early leaders were so afraid of what could happen to the highly trained mind they unwittingly missed an opportunity to teach a new generation how to maintain a powerful Pentecostal pulpit while producing a large number of respected scholars.

In the second half of the twentieth century, the Pentecostal world in America has opened its doors wider and wider to Christian higher education. Institutions of higher learning have multiplied, and the standard of education for ministry has been generally rising in almost all Pentecostal denominations. The challenge now facing the Pentecostal preacher is how to use scholarship properly within the arena of faith. Will he look to scholars for his authority, or will he use scholarship to articulate more clearly the inerrant, inspired authority of God's Holy Word? This challenge is a matter of spiritual life and death, for both the minister and those ministered to.

No scholar on earth is educated enough to question the divinity of Jesus Christ and the infallibility of Scripture. Doing so automatically disqualifies one as an authority in divine truth. One has moved from a spiritual paradigm to a carnal paradigm. The carnal mind cannot know the things of God. The source of a carnal mind is rebellion against divine truth and authority. Scholars who question the incarnate Word of God are like students in math who decide the subject is not real and its teacher merely builds lessons on false assumptions. If such a group of students persisted, several negative things would happen. Soon after dismissing math as a true science, they would begin to think it was not worth their time to learn it. Other math students would call them fools, and mathematicians would call them ignorant. Good students of math have questions about math, but they do not question the reality and value of math. In the same way, a good Bible scholar will have questions about the incarnate and written Word but will never question its reality or veracity. The Word of God sits in judgment on the student, not the other way around.

The Settled Word

Pentecostal preachers need never be ashamed of the Word they declare, because it is not in flux; it is settled. Where it may be in question is inconsequential. Long before worlds were formed, churches built, or universities and seminaries founded, the Word of God was established as the ultimate revelation of eternal, absolute truth.

Pentecostals have no problem with higher education until it discounts revelation by the Spirit of God. Science by itself is limited in understanding because all it can observe is present reality and physical processes. The revelation of the Word of God, both incarnate and written, comes first; and then comes science, higher education, and criticism.

If a person is going to preach in the twenty-first century, it is critical to know absolute truth and how it is received. That person had better know for sure the source of spiritual comprehension. That person had better know for sure that a man or woman cannot know God through human wisdom and understanding. That person had better know for sure the Word of God is to be declared, not questioned. The certainty of this position rests upon unshakeable evidence.

"All scripture is God-breathed" (2 Timothy 3:16). It does not say "Most" scripture or "Some" scripture or even "All scripture is God-breathed 'but' . . . " The statement is unqualified; it is total and conclusive. Otherwise, the Scripture would not be authoritative; at any given time it would be subject to the best opinion. Scripture would not be "settled" because nothing can be settled in the world of changing human opinion. Each opinion could be successively broken by further study and argument.

The preacher of God's Word is not doomed to sorting out what part of the Bible is inspired. He has been given the canon of Scripture, which is not composed of just a number of disconnected books but a cohesive revelation of divine quality whose source is recognized as that which could only be "God-breathed."

The Incarnate Word

Some argue the Bible cannot be the Word of God because of human instrumentality. Such an argument fails to take into account the incarnate Word used a human vessel yet remained divine, without sin or error. Furthermore, if human fallibility rules on infallible Scripture, then it follows by simple logic we cannot have any Scripture that is infallible and inerrant.

In Milan, Italy, stands one of the most breathtaking cathedrals in the world. One of the remarkable facts about it is that it took five centuries to complete—through war, famine, and the death of many workers. Yet the cathedral is obviously the design of one mind because of its symmetry and perfection. The designer was the architect—long dead; nevertheless, workers for centuries stayed true to his "inspired" drawings. The Bible was written by forty writers over hundreds of years, but the writers were only instruments in the hand of a single Architect—still alive—who breathed His Word through them and created divine perfection.

In his book *The Infallible Word,* John Murray makes a powerful observation about Paul's claim in 2 Timothy 3:16:

> Paul was, of course, well aware God used human instruments in giving us these Scriptures. In his epistles he makes repeated allusion to the human authors of the sacred books. But the recognition of human instrumentality did not in the least inhibit Paul from making the stupendous affirmation that all scripture of God is God-breathed, which means the Scripture is of divine origin and authorship and therefore of divine character and authority (The Presbyterian Guardian Publishing Corp., Philadelphia, 1946, p. 30).

Paul's claim is nothing less than the high doctrine of plenary inspiration, for Paul is not speaking of an inbreathing into the writer of the Holy Scripture by God nor even into Holy Scripture itself. The term Paul uses represents the concept of "breathing out," rather than that of "breathing in," and is far removed from the notion a human product or witness is so interpenetrated with truth or influence that it becomes the Word of God. The whole emphasis is upon the fact all Scripture proceeds from God and is therefore invested with divinity that makes it as authoritative and efficient as a word orally spoken by God directly to us.

When it comes to the Word of God, Pentecostal preachers should be convinced in their own minds; that is the area of truth in which God has especially equipped them and ordained them to study, "correctly handle" (2 Timothy 2:15), and declare. Therefore, Pentecostal preachers should embrace constant learning and take advantage of every opportunity to better themselves through higher education.

The Written Word

The written Word comes to us in the form of language. It follows that the person who wrote it intends for someone to read it. That takes literacy, a foundational aspect of education. Furthermore, if the writer authorizes another to teach the writing, then the writer must naturally desire that those who so teach understand it. That means the teacher has a responsibility to be faithful not only to what the writer wrote but also to what the writer means.

Spirit-filled scholars love God's Word so much they want not only to study texts but also to understand contexts. They want to study every uncial, phrase, sentence, and paragraph. They want to compare as many ancient manuscripts in the original languages as possible. They study customs, demographics, and archeology. Every preacher of God's Word needs to take advantage of the rich resources and products of good scholarship, not for the purpose of questioning God's Word but to be more effective in clarifying what God's Word says.

Not only should preachers have a trained mind for God to use, but they should also be trained communicators in order to proclaim God's Word more effectively to the culture and the contemporary church; thus, the need for hermeneutics, homiletics, and public speaking.

Any preacher who does not want to become more proficient, to have greater clarity, in declaring the Word stands under self-indictment. Some of the hue and cry against Christian higher education is not motivated by a legitimate fear of undermining inerrancy but by an antipathy to disciplined study.

Misusing Faith

In some cases, higher education has led to heresy. But a great danger also lies in using faith as a substitute for scholarship. The same Bible that contains "'Not by might nor by power, but by my Spirit'" (Zechariah 4:6) also contains "Study to shew thyself approved unto God" (2 Timothy 2:15, KJV) and "My people are destroyed from lack of knowledge" (Hosea 4:6). Pentecostals should not fear scholarship in and of itself any more than they should fear encouraging the gifts of the Spirit. But like all good things, higher education and criticism can be and have been misused.

It is a bit amusing to hear Pentecostals admonish the critics of speaking with tongues not to "throw out the baby with the bathwater" and then do just that with higher education. This does not mean Pentecostals should be indifferent to error in affirming scholarship or unmindful higher education tends to build pride instead of humility. Education can lead to a questioning of God rather than a questing for God; it can move us from "God has said" to "Has God said?" And if inerrancy and inspiration can be questioned, then the Scriptures are not really settled in heaven but actually subject to the educated guesses of earth.

There is no question scholars such as Renan, Strauss, and Barth had great minds and were very educated. However, they made the fatal error of sitting in judgment on the Scriptures, misusing higher criticism to support their theories instead of seeking to bring greater clarity to, and building faith in, the veracity of God's Word. For instance, Karl Barth could not understand the inspiration of Scripture by reason and logic, so he decided to make biblical inspiration conditional and subjective as opposed to authoritative and objective. The result of his struggle is a theory of logic that happens to be untrue. In his opinion, the

Bible could speak an inspired word and become the Word of God as the medium of truth, but the Scripture is not inherently inspired. Barth did not accept God's Word, so he preached his own error. If the Word of God can only be such for a particular person at a particular time, then the character of Scripture is dependent upon the circumstances of mind and environment. The results are disastrous.

The Underlying Battle: Faith vs. Reason

The underlying battle waged against inspiration and inerrancy is not higher education against the uneducated but the tension between faith and reason. The ultimate authority in the mind of a Pentecostal preacher is one's faith in the Word of God, accepting the fact that there will always be unresolved mysteries in matters of faith.

The proud heart will not accept God as the ultimate authority, so God himself is a mystery; consequently His words and works remain unknowable, unable to be understood. The darkened mind is at enmity with the revelation of God. When people do not accept authority, they do everything in their power to discredit and question it. A rebellious child will go to great lengths in resisting a parent's word, using its childish mind to point out perceived unfairness. Adults do the same with God; however, when they do not want to retain God in their knowledge they may find themselves given over to a reprobate mind (Romans 1:28).

The true scholar does not seek to prove the Bible wrong by studying perceived inconsistencies and problems. Rather, the true scholar seeks to understand the Scripture more clearly through correctly handling it, examining manuscripts, understanding custom, and appreciating archeology. In other words, the true scholar believes the limitation resides in finite minds and perceptions, not the text.

No one knows why the original autographs of Holy Scripture were not protected and retained. Perhaps in

God's wisdom He knew the Church would make them objects of worship, leading to superstitious veneration. What God did protect was the perfection of His text. One of the greatest miracles in history is the way God preserved His Word. He did not leave transference to chance. In spite of all the translations from one language to another, in spite of the various theories of translation, scholarly translations of the Scripture are amazingly consistent. Variant readings account for a very small percentage of the Scripture and in that very small percentage, not one major doctrine is negated or seriously affected.

The Issue of Translation

In recent years, a multitude of Bible translations have come to the church. Great controversy has surrounded the shift away from the King James Version as the most popular text. Pentecostal preachers can take comfort in the fact that major translations (i.e., those done with a large number of recognized scholars carefully studying the most newly discovered ancient texts along with the rich depository of manuscripts gathered through centuries) have in no way weakened the great doctrines. To the contrary, they confirm the truth with greater clarity for the modern believer.

It would be incongruous to think God, who superintended the writing of Scripture through the Holy Spirit, would allow any generation to be robbed of saving truth. His Word is a living Word. It does not change in its truth. Translations are allowed by God so the original message will not be impeded by language as the Holy Spirit anoints God's revelation. If modern translations were not true to the text of the original languages or if translators were evil, then new Bibles would strip Christ of His divinity, discount the blood, remove the miracles, and mock heaven and hell, which is not the case in any major translation recognized in evangelical circles. Of course, translators are not perfect people. The fact of imperfect human instrumentality is a greater proof the Bible is not a product of the human mind but of the Spirit of truth Himself; and in spite of changing linguistic vehicles, not one jot or tittle of God's Truth has changed on its journey to the pulpit of the modern preacher.

The Bible was written to make sense to any audience in any age. Good textual criticism is nothing more than a careful study and comparison of manuscripts. Pentecostals should never despise their continual discipline in scholarship, because the more the Word of God is studied, the more it confirms truth. "The grass withers and the flowers fall, but the word of our God stands forever" (Isaiah 40:8). It is a thrill to observe non-Pentecostal translators who are committed to accuracy, reaffirming in every translation the doctrine of the Holy Spirit, all the gifts of the Spirit, and the validity of the Pentecostal experience.

The Confirmation of Scripture

The Pentecostal preacher can expound the Scriptures as the Word of God because the Lord of the Church Himself confirmed them in His ministry while on the earth. When confronting the devil, He pled the ultimate authority: "It is written." End of argument. He proved the Sadducees in error and then gave the reason for their problem: "You are in error because you do not know the Scriptures or the power of God" (Matt 22:29, NIV). And if He had never said anything about the Word except His declaration in Luke 21:33, it would be enough to maintain faith in the Scriptures: "Heaven and earth will pass away, but my words will never pass away."

Hundreds of references in the Bible assure us we are in possession of the inerrant, inspired Word of God. The New Testament church was built upon the Word. The apostles declared the incarnate Word and appealed to the written Word as their authority. Some complain the Bible cannot prove itself by itself, using the argument you cannot accept the validity of an author based upon His own words; but in the case of the Bible, He is the only one who can validate what is inspired and infallible. In other words, God alone is the adequate witness to Himself and His Word.

The Witness of Conversion

Not only does God validate His Word by the witness of Christ and the internal witness of Scriptures themselves, but He also does so through the witness of changed lives: those who have read and believed the Word. No other book in the world can boast such results. The Complete Works of Shakespeare are recognized as one of the greatest examples of English literature, but all the reading and studying of Shakespeare cannot bring a sense of soul-cleansing and healing like the Bible does.

The preacher must never neglect the study of God's Word by replacing it with other great writings, even books based upon the Scriptures. Because the Scriptures are inspired and God-breathed, they alone can satisfy the needs of the soul and spirit. They are alive with divine inspiration.

In the classic face-off between Jesus and the devil in the wilderness, the Son of God as the Son of Man revealed the vital relationship between human beings and God's Word. Satan began his tempting of Christ with a challenge to use miracle power to meet the necessities of physical life. The devil knew the Lord had been fasting for forty days and nights and had to be famished. "If you are the Son of God, tell these stones to become bread" (Matthew 4:3). Satan tempts every preacher with similar words. "If you are full of God and called of God, then use your faith to meet the necessities of physical life and gain material possessions." Christ replied with a revelation far exceeding any insight of modern psychology: "Man [made in the image of God] does not live on bread [physical nourishment] alone, but on every word that comes from the mouth of God" (Matthew 4:4).

Pentecostal preachers need to understand that when they enter the pulpit filled with the Spirit, Word of God in hand and its message in their hearts, they are the ordained authority of God to speak life into the soul and spirit of their listeners. What a responsibility! What a privilege!

Paul's admonition to Timothy to "preach the Word" (2 Timothy 4:2) was not spoken neutrally, matter-of-factly. Paul had been the religious fanatic who ministered death before he met Christ; out of his Damascus experience came an apostle who ministered life. The hallmark of his ministry thereafter was Christ crucified and risen, based upon fulfillment of the Scriptures (1 Corinthians 15:3). So when Paul commanded Timothy what to preach, he was telling his "son in the gospel" to minister life, not death, by preaching the authoritative, life-giving Word of God.

The Question of Relevancy

One of the buzzwords in the contemporary church is "relevant." Is the church *relevant*? Is the Bible *relevant*? Is the pulpit *relevant*? The answer to that question is conditional. The church, the Bible, and the pulpit are relevant only if they are ministering spiritual life through the power of the Spirit. They are relevant only if they are fulfilling their divine purpose.

Is the church relevant? If it is seeking to minister primarily to the physical and psychological needs of its members, it is not relevant in the eyes of God. If its first concern is to attract young people to the physical church, prepare people to be successful in the world, and minister to the social and material needs of the community, it may be relevant to people but not to God.

Is the Bible relevant? If it is used as a compilation of tradition, a resource of wise sayings, a reinforcement for prejudice, a proof text for legalism, or a textbook for a reading program, it is not relevant. As a matter of fact, it can be a tool for spiritual death rather than life.

Is the pulpit relevant? If it uses the Bible simply to find a text to support a sermon outline or speaks only to popular themes and avoids "all the counsel of God" (Acts 20:27, KJV), if it is used as a hobbyhorse for an angry preacher, if it is seeking to make sinners and carnal Christians feel comfortable in the light of eternity—then the pulpit may be relevant to people but not to God.

The preacher's relevance, authority, purpose, and power are all kingdom based. In other words, his relevance is to be what is relevant to Christ. His authority is not "what people think" but "what the Lord says." His purpose is to please God first, the people second— not the other way around. His power is in the Holy Spirit, not church politics or human ability.

The living Word of God is always relevant to men and women constitutionally. One of the most poignant longings of the human heart is for authoritative guidance. Proof of this is seen by the ever-increasing popularity of the occult. Nearly every secular newspaper and magazine offers horoscopes. Books and charts on astrology are being written and promoted by a growing number of fortune-tellers, warlocks, and witches. However, the preacher has a "more sure word of prophecy" (2 Peter 1:19, KJV), which will hold up under scrutiny and lead men and women to the saving truth of Christ.

The Bible contains all the truth needed to set forth the way of salvation and Christian growth and development. It is a textbook on eternal truth but uses knowledge to underscore, illustrate, and apply divine truth for human understanding. The Bible is not a textbook on science, history, psychology, or any other educational discipline, but everything it says about these subjects is true.

The preacher must not fall into the trap of trying to defend the faith by spending an inordinate amount of time studying false religions and attacking human theories. T. F. Zimmerman, the former general superintendent of the Assemblies of God, loved to tell about a banker from the Midwest who was invited to the U.S. Mint for a weeklong seminar on how to detect counterfeit money. Upon his return, he told his friends he had never studied harder with such intensity for a week. However, they never studied one piece of counterfeit money. After a week of living with and studying the genuine, they did not need to do so. They knew the real so well the false could not deceive them.

Lifelong Learning

Preachers must be lifelong students of the Word of God for at least two reasons. First, to gain approval from God, because God is serious about the integrity of His Word. He does not want His ministers misrepresenting or mishandling the truth of the Scriptures. Second, to avoid losing integrity as interpreters of the Word. Ministers who are not serious students of the Bible eventually bring shame to themselves and a reproach to their calling.

The goal of biblical study is to bring the truth of God to the human race. That is accomplished by "accurately handling the word of truth" (2 Timothy 2:15). The proper use of hermeneutics is of great value in guarding against improper interpretation, especially in application. For instance, a good hermeneutic will help the preacher divide illustrative truth from absolute truth.

It is quite clear the absolute truth of spiritual humility is illustrated by washing feet. Jesus was teaching His disciples they were not above menial tasks. Some have focused on the statement "You also should wash one another's feet" (John 13:14) as not only the truth being set forth by Jesus but also an ordinance to be practiced by the church. The greater application, however, is love, not law. The disciples in that day of open sandals and dusty feet were to routinely wash feet. In our day, the illustration itself does not apply; it is not a custom of hospitality. However, having the loving and humble heart of a servant remains as the absolute truth, in our day translating perhaps into a willingness to cut the grass, serve tables, pick up people for church, straighten up the sanctuary after communion, and so forth.

In the culture where Paul was ministering, braided hair on women was a symbol of great pride; it was often used by the wealthy to display jewels and expensive ornaments. In writing Timothy, Paul taught against ostentatious display (1 Timothy 2:9). Today, however, the illustration referring to braided hair makes very little sense. If Paul were alive today, he would still preach the truth of modesty and temperance but would use other illustrations. The same would hold true regarding women keeping silent in the congregation. We know from correctly handling the Word of truth women were filled with the Spirit, prophesied, and taught. Paul was using an illustrative truth or circumstance to teach order and respect in corporate worship.

Much care must be taken under the supervision of the Holy Spirit by any proclaimer of the Word of God. It is the greatest of all responsibilities to be "stewards of the mysteries of God" (1 Corinthians 4:1, KJV); let us not be guilty of preaching "self" but faithfully preach Christ and His Word.

The Spirit and the Word

Thank God, the preacher is not without divine help in discharging the grave responsibility of proclaiming the gospel. The reign of the Holy Spirit and the preaching of God's Word are providentially linked in order to reveal, illuminate, and apply the Word through God's called ones.

By being open to the Spirit's anointing upon their minds and hearts, Pentecostal preachers can be greatly benefited in both study and proclamation. The same Spirit who raised Christ from the dead quickens our mortal bodies, and the same Spirit who breathed inspiration and divine truth through the writers of the Word is available to reveal to the preacher what God is saying in and through His Scriptures.

Pentecostals are not exempt from error and should be especially careful not to stray from the Word of God. For example, if left unchecked and not brought under the authority of the Word of God, vocal gifts can open the door to a false interpretation of truth.

For some time, the charismatic/Pentecostal world

has used the term "rhema word." In the purest sense, the Holy Scripture is the *rhema* word, but can God and does God give the church an inspired Word not in the language of the Bible? Certainly! But in its meaning and purpose that Word is subject to the inerrant Word. The danger comes in elevating a *rhema* word to the level of Scripture. Be assured, all the dreams, visions, *rhema* words, and prophetic utterances will never add to or change the Word of God. Under the anointing of the Holy Spirit, they will simply bring revelational truth to what is written.

The Word of the Lord is to be proclaimed by men and women ordained by God and filled with the Holy Spirit. The results of being faithful to that Word fill many books with glorious testimonies in the library of Pentecost. May we again believe that as the Word is preached, wonderful signs and wonders will follow. May again the Pentecostal pulpit believe sin's power is broken by the truth of salvation even as the Word is declared. May again the Pentecostal pulpit believe the Lord will send His Word in healing as the preacher delivers the good news in the authority of Jesus' name and the anointing of the Holy Spirit.

Chapter 4
The Jesus Model

Jesus was the first Pentecostal preacher. All of the elements of a Spirit-filled, empowered minister are prominent in His earthly ministry. He is the ultimate role model of all God-ordained ministers.

But the value in studying Jesus as a preacher will not be discovered in His historical model alone. The preacher must seek to grasp and apply the dynamic, timeless principles He practiced. In fact, the content and style of His life and ministry are instructive and critical to every disciple of Christ in all ages. However, it is what Jesus set in motion as a recruiter, instructor, and role model in ministry that is most germane to the ordained preacher.

Remember, Jesus did not go to the cross the moment He entered the public arena. He had much to do to establish the Church. It would be the continual expression of His body on the earth. Jesus came not only to die for the establishing of His Church but also to model a life and ministry for its members—especially those He would call and ordain to lead after His time on earth was finished.

Secure Identity

Jesus knew who He was. This fact is not incidental but foundational. It was the source of His authority and thus His security. Nowhere in scripture can a student find where Jesus ever questioned His identity. This fact gave Him the strength to explain His conduct

59

to Mary and Joseph at the age of 12, overcome the temptation of the devil, confront religious leaders, be patient with His disciples, face hardships and poverty, and go to the cross.

An insecure preacher cannot be effective in contemporary America. Unless he knows who he is in relation to God and clearly understands the meaning of a divine ordination, he will be destroyed by a convergence of negative pressures. As with all others before him, the modern preacher is going to have to be secure enough to overcome Satan's temptation of material gain in exchange for a diminished ministry, resist spiritual pride, and reject short-term positive gains at the expense of long-term negative consequences. In addition, the new generation of American preachers will need to stand firmly against a post-modern, non-Christian culture.

Because Jesus was secure, He spoke His message with authority and embraced all who believed in Him. The immense popularity of John could have been a threat to an insecure preacher, but Jesus sought him out publicly to request his baptism. John was very different from Christ; his methodologies were at times bizarre. Yet Jesus did not criticize him. John's imprisonment could have been an opportunity for a less-than-secure peer to secretly gloat. Some might have said, "If John's ministry had been valid or if he had used a bit more wisdom, he would not find himself in this situation." Christ, however, modeled for everyone in the ministry the debt owed to those who have been and are presently preaching the gospel. He said of John: "Among those born of women there has not risen anyone greater than John the Baptist" (Matthew 11:11). The Church would be much stronger and more effective if all her ministers reacted to fellow ministers as Christ did.

Our Lord was secure as well in the truth He embodied and proclaimed. He revealed an awesome knowledge of God and theology at an early age. Some will argue no human being could be expected to have the grasp and scope of knowledge Jesus had because of His divine nature. On the other hand, He emptied himself of many supernatural abilities to reveal truth in the flesh. The degree of Christ's knowledge of theology and religion may not be a realistic goal, but the priority He placed upon these matters serves as an inspiration and directive to the preacher. The Christian minister, by definition, must be a lifelong student of the Word of God and Bible doctrine, or he will lose his identity as a preacher of truth.

Handpicked Leadership

Jesus' ministry revealed another great priority. If anyone doubts the importance of the preacher and the pulpit from heaven's point of view, all they need to do is note the time and effort Jesus put into ministerial recruitment and development. Heaven's strategy was not to send Christ to earth to build His Church by divine coup but to put in place the process and methodology through which He would build His Church. The importance of leadership is not a new concept; it is a divine principle. It is so important God still handpicks and guides His leaders.

As a sidelight upon God's recruitment program, all serious students of the first-century class of 12 have shaken their collective heads at the kind of men God called. For that matter, the best of church leaders often question if God is still calling misfits and disqualified people to be His voice on eternal matters. Perhaps it is because the wise, the mighty, and the noble find it difficult to accept such a call; their sufficiency and security are often in their gifts and abilities rather than in Christ.

The world believes education is the first criteria to success, human ability the first runner-up, and good connections the second runner-up. If the Church adopts this same criteria, it will consider many God has ordained as unfit and unqualified. Notice, Jesus first called His disciples and then trained them. Too often the modern church prepares candidates for the pulpit using a secular curriculum based upon human accreditation and then decides whether they should be ordained based upon their ability to pass an academic standard.

Without a doubt, the Holy Spirit will guide God's ordained to seek a good education, not for the purpose of qualifying them for ministry, however, but to make them more effective in the culture. Formal education by its very nature can undermine a supernatural ministry, tempting the preacher to move his dependency from God to human ability. (God's ministers have always been asked to do the impossible.)

The task of the modern preacher is the same Jesus imposed upon His own ministry: "'The Spirit of the Lord is on me, because he has anointed me to preach good news to the poor. He has sent me to proclaim freedom for the prisoners and recovery of sight for the blind, to release the oppressed, to proclaim the year of the Lord's favor'" (Luke 4:18-19). This is one of the most remarkable statements in Scripture; Jesus confesses that the effectiveness of His ministry is not in His divinity but in His anointing. Now every preacher can adopt the same goals of a "Jesus ministry," complete with supernatural deliverance. Every preacher is a candidate for the same enduement of power from on high—the anointing of the Holy Spirit.

At the same time God anoints, He seeks humility in those He calls. In so doing, He has had to crush human pride so His anointed find no confidence in their human ability. Moses was trained in all the wisdom of Egypt. At 40, he decided he was capable of a deliverance ministry using his own prowess and power. The result was a 40-year exile from any influence or input into the Egyptian captivity. He became so capable in his own eyes, God couldn't use him. After 40 years of eating humble pie, he received God's summons, "Now, go deliver your people." Moses immediately said, "I can't. I don't have any self-confidence. I don't have the people skills. I don't have the connections. I don't have the resources, and I've been talking to sheep so long I can't communicate with humans." Moses was so void of human dependence and ability God could now flow through him unhindered.

A good education for ministry is wonderful until it is misused, until we attempt to do the humanly impossible with it. It is like a highly educated man who comes upon an accident victim being crushed to death under a fallen tree. There is nothing wrong with the would-be deliverer having a good education, but it does not give him supernatural strength to lift the tree and set the victim free.

If the preacher ever thinks he can fulfill the Great Commission, destroy the works of the devil, and set men and women free through better education and communication alone, he is doomed to failure. When it came to ministry, the apostle Paul put all his achievements on the dung heap. He recognized that total dependence upon God was the only hope for an effective life and ministry.

Kingdom Authority

The goal of Christ's ministry determined the content of His message. It was the proclamation of the kingdom of God, that is, the authority and rule of God over humanity. That authority astonished the people who heard Him. They sensed it was from another source than that of the scribes and Pharisees, for they derived any influence they had from religious tradition and political intrigues.

Jesus not only revealed the goal of a divine ministry, but He also clarified the roles of human and divine government. This distinction needs to be constantly put forward by the preacher. Jesus never displaced human government or distinctive cultures. He knew their place and insisted those who followed Him do the same (see Mark 12:17 and Matthew 17:27).

Jesus' comfort level with human government will surprise those who study His model of ministry. He does no ranting or raving against the deplorable, spiritually bankrupt emperor or his laws. He demanded His disciples obey the law of the land and pay taxes. He honored rulers as being in authority over temporal government so people could live peaceable lives. He understood the role of the temporal.

When authority became an issue, Jesus very succinctly explained His rule was over a kingdom not of this world; His kingdom was spiritual and eternal. Neither He nor His disciples would fight to become political rulers. His subjects were no threat to temporal rulers. To the contrary, the noble qualities of a good citizen were refined by the internal work of the Spirit, ultimately producing the kind of person any king would want as a subject.

It is a bit mystifying to hear the modern pulpit misapply the laws of God and men—as well as the role of culture. The role of the pulpit is to declare the supreme authority of God in all of His power and glory, not reject authority ordained by God to rule over nations.

Cultural Relevance

Jesus' message is one of spiritual authority, not cultural relevance. He showed us there is nothing wrong with cultural relevance, but only to illustrate truth, not to seek it. To do otherwise is to assign too great a value to the temporary, resulting in compromising eternal absolutes. Jesus used parables to reveal truth. He connected immediately with the woman at the well by using the relevancy of the moment (a woman seeking water) to make the message spiritually and eternally relevant (superior water). He was eternally relevant to the rich young ruler by demanding he sell what he had and give it to the poor. He was telling the young man to surrender the most precious thing in his culture to gain wealth in an eternal kingdom and a spiritual culture. The young man refused to part with his material kingdom in order to become a ruler in an eternal kingdom. He went away sorrowful because he could not reconcile the proper place of two kingdoms. He wanted to keep one kingdom at the cost of another. He wanted to please two masters when one challenged the other.

What has all this got to do with a preacher in the twenty-first century? The rich, the successful, the powerful are saying, "If you can craft your message to appeal to me, I'll listen. If I can be a good Christian and keep my world under my control, okay. If the message from the pulpit does not threaten my business or lifestyle, I'll go for it. If you tell me my religion will interfere with my world, forget it."

Today we would identify the rich young ruler as a highly successful member of the Buster generation, concerned about life after death and what adjustments he would have to make in order to be considered a good Christian. But Jesus would carefully explain he could have eternal life if he would be willing to be an entrepreneur under God's rule. The price? The surrender of a temporal empire. The creed of the eternal kingdom says the greatest success is found in servanthood: "It is more blessed to give than to receive" (Acts 20:35). To find purpose and meaning in life, you have to surrender what you know and own and come under the rule of His authority. The world you are trying to gain and keep is not an end in itself. It is a divine provision for the moment. It is worth nothing in comparison to what you will gain by seeking God's kingdom and His righteousness first.

Jesus was quite comfortable with the temporal because it was not vital to Him in relation to His mission. He was not beholden to any world authority for His ministry—as no ordained preacher of the gospel should be. The world should never give the man of God his cues. He is to be utterly under the authority of God's kingdom. Can you imagine Jesus saying to Himself: "I must not say anything to offend this very fine successful young ruler" or "I must be relevant and offer the woman at the well a new or better method to draw water" or "I need to get on the board of the temple so I can use my influence to have them consider moving the money tables to a less intrusive spot"?

The Jesus model shows the preacher how to respond to the whole matter of authority. There is no need to be threatened or unduly affected by the culture. It is never to be a controlling factor in a bona fide gospel ministry. However, the preacher must address the culture as a known reality and as a means to lead men and women to God and eternal life.

Responsible to People

The authority of Jesus was applied in His ministry not by being responsible *for* people but by being responsible *to* people. You can only be responsible for one part of a relationship—your own. The fear of people sets a dangerous trap, especially for contemporary preachers.

Jesus was never responsible for people. If He had been, everyone He ministered to would have been saved, healed, and perfected. Instead, Jesus was responsible *to* people. He presented truth in love. He did everything He could to offer people the benefits of salvation. When He did so, His responsibility was finished; what He offered then became the individual's responsibility.

Many pulpits are rendered ineffective because the preachers who fill them are trying to be responsible for how a certain individual or group might react. It does not take much insight to see the results of such mental anguish. The preacher will begin to avoid such critical subjects as moral depravity because people might think he is attacking their self-image. Abortion—because the daughter of an important member had one. Divorce—because people will think the preacher is insensitive to single-parent homes. Hell and the lake of fire—because people will think the minister is old-fashioned and uneducated. The list goes on and on until in the minds of the listener the need for a new birth has been nullified.

Responsible for Truth

Today's pulpit must be responsible to the American people. The preacher is responsible to preach the truth, the whole truth, and nothing but the truth—God's truth. He is responsible to preach with love and compassion. He is responsible to prepare his message with untiring effort and skill. When he has been faithful to the people, his responsibility is ended. It then becomes the responsibility of the hearer to respond.

Jesus told His disciples to be responsible to the people of all the communities they entered by preaching the truth. If the people responded favorably and embraced salvation, the disciples were to joyfully establish them in the faith. If they responded unfavorably, the disciples were to wipe the dust off their feet as they left the village to signify they had fulfilled their responsibility. The response, with all its attendant consequences, was now the responsibility of the inhabitants.

Paul warned Timothy a mark of the last days would be people not putting up with sound doctrine. They would search for preachers who would preach cleverly but not faithfully. That audience would consist of people just "itching" to hear an entertaining communicator, one not so much interested in their relationship to God as in pleasing a crowd.

The preacher must never prepare a message with the thought of what the people want to hear but rather what God wants to say. The preacher is responsible first and foremost to the Lord and then to the people. This gives to the one ordained tremendous freedom for fulfilling his responsibility in the pulpit.

Communication Styles of Jesus

Talking Truth

The communication styles of Jesus are most interesting. He was comfortable in sharing truth in every venue and adjusted His style accordingly.

The first style is not preaching but conversation. An important element in the ministry is the ability to talk the gospel. Jesus modeled this style, showing His disciples a "congregation" of one was worth their best effort. Two great examples of Christ's conversations were those with Nicodemus and the woman at the well. Some of the most outstanding evangelistic sermons of all time have been built upon the truths in Jesus' conversations with these two people.

The effective proclaimer of the gospel must be an effective communicator of the gospel one-on-one. Truth proclaimed to a crowd begins with truth proclaimed to individuals who happen to form a group. Great preachers will advise their students to preach to an individual, not a crowd. Those who work in radio and television helping communicators focus what they are saying train them not to think of the masses but to think of one person listening to the radio or watching the TV. The goal of all gospel communication is to bring people—one at a time—to a decision after they have been confronted with the truth.

In a day of mass media, demographics, social studies, and group psychology, the preacher can lose the individual in the public arena. The overall ministry of Christ cannot help but impress the student with how much time and effort He expended on one person. It could never be said of Jesus, "He loved crowds but hated people." At Pentecost we are introduced to mass evangelism and multiple conversions, but Christ's evangelism was often connected to one-on-one contexts, when He talked the gospel.

Teaching Truth

The second communication style of Christ was teaching. He taught the gospel of the kingdom. He often taught great crowds of people over comparatively long periods of time. On one occasion, He taught a multitude for three days. It takes time to teach the great truths of the kingdom.

The teaching style of Christ challenges the modern preacher. In a culture on a merciless treadmill, how can quality time to make disciples be provided? Many throw up their hands in surrender to the multiple demands upon them, thinking the answer is to provide less time for teaching instead of more.

However, the famine of the Word of God in America today has exceptions, proving an anointed pulpit teacher can overcome our culture's demands on time. Some of the fastest growing and most stable congregations are built upon strong, frequent Bible teaching and expositional preaching. The hunger for God's Word is not cultural but constitutional; thus, those preachers who concentrate on exposition with competency and authority will attract and hold spiritually hungry people.

Jesus ministered in a morally decadent age (what age is not?). He had to confront a dominating, dead religious leadership. The political atmosphere was equally dominating and intrusive. Nevertheless, crowds were drawn by the great exposition and spiritual insights of the Master Teacher. Pentecostal preachers must avoid the temptation to build a church or ministry by the sensational and spectacular. After all the tricks have been played and rabbits pulled out of the hat, the crowds will leave seeking a better religious show; but the faithful teacher-preacher of the Word will ultimately feed the Lord's flock and build the church.

Proclaiming Truth

The third communication style of Christ was preaching. He not only taught the people but also "preached the gospel" (Luke 20:1). Jesus was a powerful proclaimer of "good news." Following His baptism and temptation, He defined what He was by what He did: "From that time Jesus began to preach" (Matthew 4:17). He instructed His disciples to preach: "As you go, preach this message: 'The kingdom of heaven is near'" (Matthew 10:7). His final instructions to those He ordained and anointed were clear: "Go into all the world and preach the good news to all creation" (Mark 16:15). Jesus, by His example, put in motion for those He called the never-ending importance and priority of preaching.

The Pentecostal preacher who seeks to follow Christ's model needs to note He addressed the obstacles and barriers that prevented the proclamation of the gospel. A great number of His messages are warnings against false religion and its consequences for those who practiced it. He did not hesitate to cry out against the Pharisees and Sadducees in public—in their presence. He saw them as enemies of the truth who needed to be confronted. Jesus was an uncompromising apologist. Those who mishandled divine truth drew His righteous indignation, nor could He remain silent when those who needed the truth were lied to in the name of truth. Part of the preacher's task in modern America is to stand up and warn the people of false doctrine and corrupt religion in a day of corrupted truth.

The prophetic voices of the twenty-first century will speak loudly and clearly against a false ecumenicism in the name of Christian love and tolerance. One of the great deceptions of the last days will be a misuse of Jesus' prayer for unity in the body of Christ: "That they may be one, as we are one" (John 17:11). The deception comes into play when unity becomes a goal by any means.

A minister received an advertisement about a new church beginning in his area. It contained an appeal to anyone of any religious faith—Catholic, Protestant, Jew, Muslim, Hindu—to be a Sunday school teacher. It made no difference because this new church recognized all faiths as equal and rejected divisive dogma. In the interest of unity, modern ecumenists have a great desire to ignore doctrine. Anything that divides is viewed as evil—especially doctrine.

Even so, there is one true Church, and Jesus Christ is building that Church. It is built upon the unity of God the Father and God the Son and God the Holy Spirit. It is a Church of which Jesus Christ is the chief cornerstone. It is a Church of one Lord, one faith, one baptism—and if an angel preaches any other gospel than that based upon the good news of Calvary, the resurrection, and the eternal reign of Christ, says Paul, "Let him be accursed" (Galatians 1:8). Let the minister of the gospel promote the unity of all believers around the person and work of Christ but stand firm against an ecumenism that embraces a faith apart from the great Bible doctrines.

Prophetic Preaching

The same questions Jesus faced and was expected to answer are the same ones confronting the preacher today: "How can a person be born again?" "Why suffering?" "What is truth?" "What follows death?" And most assuredly: "When is the end of all things?"

If a preacher has a desire to model his ministry after Christ, he should include a strong emphasis on the doctrine of last things. A very large portion of the Lord's preaching and teaching was centered upon eschatology. If the truth were known, relatively few pulpits would be viewed as strong on the subject. In addition to the importance Christ placed upon eschatology in His preaching, a special blessing is promised to anyone who reads and understands the prophecy of Revelation. Could it be that a true revival of the pulpit in America would have as one of its hallmarks a renewed interest and preaching on prophecy?

There is a special prophetic anointing inherent in the call of God and the fullness of the Spirit. Prophecy in all of its dimensions is given special attention by the Holy Spirit throughout both the Old and New Testaments, with unique guidance to the church.

The same anointing which made Christ's preaching so effective is the same anointing that will give the Spirit-filled preacher ability in prophetic forthtelling. Much anointed preaching is really prophecy in the sense of special knowledge, divine authority, and warning. Pentecostal preachers testify to times in preparation and proclamation when they were moved beyond themselves by the force of the Holy Spirit. In those moments, they were the prophetic mouthpieces of God to their generation.

Prophecy as a gift of the Holy Spirit is so important

and necessary for the church it is singled out as a priority: "Follow the way of love and eagerly desire spiritual gifts, *especially the gift of prophecy*" (1 Corinthians 14:1, NIV, my emphasis). An authentic Pentecostal church will not only covet and emphasize the gift of prophecy, but it will also be a dominant element within the life of the church.

At the dawning of the twenty-first century, there is a general consensus among Pentecostal leaders and scholars that eschatology verges on becoming de-emphasized. If that is true, the Pentecostal preacher must reckon it as a threat to a Christ-centered ministry and a sin against the church.

Understandably, many Pentecostal preachers have been turned off by so-called prophetic teachers and authors who live in the realm of speculation and have made ridiculous "prophecies," which have proven false. Other preachers have shunned the subject of prophecy because of great debates among scholars concerning timelines, the meaning of the Great Tribulation, and signs of the times. Many sincere preachers have thrown up their hands and said, "If these scholars cannot figure it out and agree, who am I to address the subject!"

Given such confusion surrounding Bible prophecy, the devil, we may assume, must be very pleased. Anything that keeps believers from looking for and anticipating the rapture of the church and the Second Coming of Christ plays into his hands.

Preacher, do not rob the church of the Blessed Hope through neglect! The only way to overcome evil is to preach the truth in the power of the Spirit. The Pentecostal preacher is not to "minister questions" (1 Timothy 1:4, KJV), which includes prophecy. He is to declare what Christ proclaimed. He is duty bound to declare the imminent return of Christ and to warn his people of the spirit of anti-Christ.

A minister need not be known as a scholar of eschatology; but by the very nature of his calling, he must rise above speculation, deny fear, and proclaim a "more sure word of prophecy" (2 Peter 1:19, KJV).

Jesus himself, the very spirit of prophecy, did so. He asks no less of His preachers. As a matter of fact, any believer who studies the Book of Revelation is promised a special blessing: "Blessed is the one who reads the words of this prophecy, and blessed are those who hear it" (1:3).

With Signs Following

Finally, the Jesus model of ministry was accompanied by miracles. If Jesus Christ were among us today, He would be holding salvation/healing crusades all over the world. What the mighty ministers of the Old Testament started, Jesus confirmed constantly as He preached. Even before Pentecost, the Lord commissioned His disciples to do the miraculous as they went forth to preach and minister. In truth, the disciples were thrilled with the divine enablement to heal the sick and cast out devils. Of course, Jesus had to teach them the proper place and priority of the miraculous in the context of salvation, but a correction of an emphasis does not negate its importance.

The Pentecostal preacher in the twenty-first century must never be satisfied with a "signless" ministry. He is charged with perpetuating a Jesus ministry through the anointing Jesus possessed. When the Pentecostal preacher preaches salvation, he can believe the sinner will become a saint. When he preaches holiness, he can expect believers to be convicted by the Spirit and change habits and lifestyles. When he preaches on the baptism of the Holy Spirit, he can expect people to receive the gift of the Holy Spirit with the initial physical evidence of speaking with other tongues. When he preaches divine healing, he can expect blind eyes to open, deaf ears to unstop, cancers to shrivel and die, and the lame to leap and walk.

The Great Commission of the Lord is center stage before the backdrop of power. "All authority in heaven and on earth has been given to me. Therefore go and make disciples of all nations, baptizing them in the name of the Father and of the Son and of the Holy

Spirit" (Matthew 28:18-19). He promises the preacher divine adequacy. He expects His ministers to do greater works. He desires to see every pulpit, every church, a part of building a mighty force for God in the final days of human history.

The Jesus model is not set before preachers as an impossibility, to raise the level of their frustration; it is set before them to put a heavenly hunger and divine drive in their souls to be more like Jesus, in both character and effectiveness. The Lord is saying to His spokesmen: "I am not only challenging you to be all you can be through my grace but also to be all you can be through my anointing and my power— Go therefore!"

Chapter 5
The Pauline Model—
Part One

Pentecostal preachers should always be constantly striving for excellence, open to change, and alert to what God is doing through others. However, they should pick their role models and "heroes" with prayerful deliberation. Without a doubt, the apostle Paul was the complete Pentecostal preacher. It has often been said that apart from Jesus Christ, no other man had a greater impact upon the Church. Consequently, preachers should carefully study and emulate Paul's preaching and ministry, while at the same time noting his humility: "Follow my example, as I follow the example of Christ" (1 Corinthians 11:1).

One of the least understood skills in preaching and pastoring is the ability to learn from the examples and methods of others without compromising personal uniqueness and Pentecostal principles.

Very few preachers have the ability to align modern methods with biblical principles. Very few Pentecostal preachers know how to adopt non-Pentecostal models without undermining Pentecostal truth. Furthermore, few Pentecostal preachers know how to visit a Pentecostal revival without trying to duplicate its effects before seeking its causes. For example, during the 1990s many ministers visited the Pensacola, Florida, revival, returned to their churches, copied the same worship style—trying to orchestrate the same responses—and failed miserably. Such preachers did not take into account the years of fasting and prayer that preceded the revival. Revival displaced God, who chooses to revive His Church however He will, very seldom through formulas.

When Paul is studied, the great principles of a timeless Pentecostal ministry surface, instead of a passing methodology. Great churches are built by pastors who follow great principles under the guidance of the Holy Spirit. Like unprincipled lives, unprincipled ministries are doomed, not anchored upon the eternal rock of our salvation but built on the quicksand of relativism.

What follows is an outline of some of the principles that explain Paul's effectiveness. Of course, these do not exhaust the marvelous characteristics Paul exemplified, but they can be and should be adopted by every minister of the gospel.

Certain of His Call

Paul was a great Pentecostal preacher because he never doubted his call. Without pride he walked in spiritual authority. A man of deep conviction, he lived without compromise. Despite the obstacles such a life can encounter, he maintained the joy of the Lord and the fruit of the Spirit.

The root of Paul's confidence can be traced to his conversion. It would be difficult to appreciate Paul without taking into account his Damascus Road experience. The Hebrew of Hebrews, the zealous Pharisee who killed Christians with a vengeance, was himself violently arrested, perhaps giving him both a sample of his own treatment of believers and something to think about in his blindness. Paul's conversion experience was so transforming it changed everything about him, even his name. If anyone could speak with authority in describing salvation as "a new creation" in Christ Jesus (2 Corinthians 5:17), it was Paul. His old life passed away in a moment and everything became new.

The authority in the pulpit begins with the preacher's transforming encounter with Jesus Christ.

The experience is not usually as spectacular as Paul's (indeed, many preachers are converted and called as children), but the results most assuredly need to be the same. If Saul of Tarsus (the old creation) had not been changed by the Spirit's revelation of Christ, the Church would never have been introduced to Paul the apostle (the new creation).

The Pentecostal pulpit is founded on the gospel. The preacher is a witness to the gospel message that results in personal salvation. There is little authority and less power in a theory or a philosophy or even a religion; however, the objective truth of the gospel furnishes a surplus of both. That is the reason redeemed people were called to be the proclaimers of the gospel instead of angels. Salvation is the preacher's "know so" experience that brings personal validity to his message.

From the moment Paul was saved, he was called to preach. In Paul's mind, he was saved not only to be a witness, as all believers are called to be, but also to be a preacher, a minister, and an apostle.

Acts 26:16-18 makes it clear Paul at the time of his salvation was not only confronted by Christ, he was also put on notice he was to be a minister and a witness of his Damascus Road experience. Furthermore, he was told his influence and responsibility would reach beyond the Jewish community by reason of his divine appointment as an apostle to the gentiles.

Paul's conversion and ordination reveal a tremendous truth. Jesus Christ saves by a variety of means and circumstances, but He saves completely. Sinners become saints, and the Spirit bears witness they are children of God. In like manner, Jesus Christ ordains men and women by a variety of means and circumstances, but He calls them so clearly they receive an unquestioned certainty. How quickly that certainty is established—whether instantly or over a period of time—is not important. God calls His ministers to preach His gospel in His own way and time, but He leaves no doubt as to that calling.

Like no other in recent memory, the twenty-first century preacher is going to need the confirmation of God's call to preach. The clouds of demonic hatred against fundamental Christianity in America are gathering at an alarming rate. Opposition to the righteous laws of God will put any true proclaimer of divine truth in the crosshairs of the enemy. Without a doubt, they will need the assurance of a certain call from an authority above human government.

Paul had no question about his call: "I was appointed a preacher and an apostle" (1 Timothy2:7, NKJV). And again, "I was appointed a preacher, an apostle, and a teacher of the Gentiles" (2 Timothy 1:11, NKJV). It is clear he held his appointment and ordination to preach in very high regard. As a matter of fact, the preaching of the gospel consumed his life. In 1 Corinthians 9:16, he makes a statement that should be echoed by every preacher of the gospel: "Woe to me if I do not preach the gospel!"

A Christ-Centered Focus

Paul was a great Pentecostal preacher because he maintained a Christ-centered focus both in life and in ministry. "For I resolved to know nothing while I was with you except Jesus Christ and him crucified" (1 Corinthians 2:2).

If Paul were to return to the contemporary scene and be given an opportunity to address every gospel preacher in America, his entire theme and message would be, "Preach Christ! Preach Christ!" The Bible record backs up this assumption; no one stayed on target with his message, or "on message," like the apostle Paul.

There is no doubt as to the central theme and subject in the record of Paul's preaching. The sermon he preached in Antioch (Acts 13:16 ff.) is a Christocentric masterpiece—a wonderful example of his preaching style and ministry. (It followed the same pattern and emphasis as Peter's sermon on the Day of Pentecost [see chapter 9].) Addressing a synagogue audience, he began his message with an oral history of the Jews.

He reminded them God had been at work in their past. As Christ did in His preaching, so Paul did also: they first found common ground and then set forth divine truth and revelation. This approach is critical to effective preaching because it keeps the preacher from losing either audience or message. Presenting new truth without the context of the familiar is futile. On the other hand, if the central purpose of the message is not focused on Christ, then preaching has become an end in itself.

The modern preacher can learn a great deal from Paul about staying on message in preaching. Paul did not allow anything to dilute, divert, or distract from the centrality of Christ, in either his preaching or his life.

Paul's statement in 1 Corinthians 1:14 is startling outside of its context: "I am thankful that I did not baptize any of you except Crispus and Gaius" (1 Corinthians 1:14). Paul seems to be diminishing the importance of baptism. In context, however, Paul is illustrating the importance of his preaching. God did not call him to baptize but to preach. Although Paul baptized, he was careful not to allow baptism to overshadow the preaching of the cross. Knowing the Corinthian church and their tendency to elevate the sensual and the material above the spiritual, he chose not to emphasize baptism as a part of his ministry; he feared they might misunderstand the purpose of baptism and see it as an identification with the one who baptized rather than with Christ. They were babes in understanding and could not correctly apply the doctrines of baptism without a greater grasp of its purpose and place. Because of this, Paul assigned others to baptize. He knew and understood the emphasis and timing of the Holy Spirit in light of the spiritual condition of the church.

My father was a dyed-in-the-wool Pentecostal preacher who loved to preach on the baptism in the Holy Spirit and then lead people into the experience. He felt led of the Lord to pioneer a church in a small community in Canada. God blessed his efforts, and in just a few weeks, a large number came to faith in Christ. He was all set to preach on the baptism of the Spirit but was strongly forbidden by the Spirit to do so. For over six months, he was restrained from preaching on the baptism. Then one night at the altar, three men were instantly filled with the Spirit and began to speak in tongues—without any word, let alone instruction, from the pulpit. The Spirit of God was leading my father's congregation into all truth and knew this baby church had not been ready to receive the truth of the baptism without getting off message, that is, Jesus Christ and Him crucified.

In the exercise of spiritual gifts, Pentecostals must guard against losing their Christocentric focus; these gifts are supernatural and rather than lead to a greater revelation of Jesus, they can fast become ends in themselves. Paul's theology of the Holy Spirit is clearly centered on Christ.

Would Paul be pleased with contemporary Pentecostal preaching? Of course, no one can answer that question definitively, but it would not be hard to imagine he would be thrilled by pulpits that always proclaimed Christ and presented the message of salvation clearly.

However, he would be incensed by Pentecostal preachers who draw attention to themselves with histrionics. After all, like John the Baptist, the preacher is not to point to himself but to another; the preacher is a servant. Paul would be angry with preachers who demand big paychecks or beg for money to line their own pockets. He was so careful not to misuse money he remained bi-vocational at the peak of his ministry. He taught the churches to give and made it clear the preacher should receive enough to live off the ministry. At the same time, he would be appalled to see preachers so greedy that where they preach can be influenced by how much money they are promised. The great strength of Paul's ministry was in his insatiable desire to be faithful to the gospel. He resolved that nothing would deter him from making Jesus Christ preeminent.

His whole life was Christ centered: "I no longer live, but Christ lives in me" (Galatians 2:20). His doctrine all pointed to Christ. His preaching was focused on Christ. It would be well for every Pentecostal preacher to remember that the call, appointment, and ordination to the ministry are the same as that of the apostle Paul's. To preach any other gospel brings a curse. To preach anything but Christ is to be off message and disobedient to the heavenly vision.

A Demonstration of Power

Paul was a great Pentecostal preacher because his preaching was not just a logical argument but also a demonstration of the power of God. It is at this point we come to the crux of Pentecostal preaching.

First Corinthians 2:1-5 is the Pentecostal preacher's manifesto. Every word should be emblazoned on the mind and lived out in every detail, from the prayer room and study to the pulpit:

> When I came to you, brothers, I did not come with elo-quence or superior wisdom as I proclaimed to you the testimony about God. For I resolved to know nothing while I was with you except Jesus Christ and him cruci-fied. I came to you in weakness and fear, and with much trembling. My message and my preaching were not with wise and persuasive words, but with a demonstration of the Spirit's power, so that your faith might not rest on men's wisdom, but on God's power.

The great challenge in the mind of Paul was to preach in such a way his hearers would center their faith on the power of God, not on human wisdom. This goal could be accomplished only by an observable demonstration of the supernatural by the Holy Spirit.

In a sense, Paul is telling all Pentecostal preachers their goal in the pulpit is impossible to achieve by human genius or ability because the goal is to change the object of people's faith from a belief system anchored in human rationale to a revelation of Christ through the ministry of the Holy Spirit.

The great apostle was transparent with the Corinthians. They were a rather sophisticated and carnal crowd who thought eloquence was a necessity and human wisdom the basis for relevance in the pulpit. They were also much taken with logic, making his statements in 1 Corinthians 2 all the more surprising. A crucified Jesus presented by a person who confessed to "weakness and fear, . . . with much trembling" does not sound like an ideal résumé.

Paul had superior education, great communicative skills, and unusual wisdom; but when he approached the pulpit, he viewed all such attainments as crutches. He said no to every human ability as the source of spiritual effectiveness and yes to a total dependence on the Holy Spirit, because he knew human ingenuity could not accomplish what needed to be done from the pulpit in the hearts and lives of those who listened.

Creating a New Person in Christ

The goal of the preacher is to be a tool used by the Holy Spirit for creating a new person in Christ, not a nice person for church membership. Preachers are to do more than articulate problems; they are to solve them through God. They are not only to diagnose diseases but also to heal them through Christ's authority. It is only through the demonstration of God's power by His Word people will change the basis of their faith from the natural to the supernatural.

All things being equal, the measure of a person's faith ought to correspond to the object of that faith. For instance, a rickety old chair does not inspire much in the way of faith. Human wisdom says, "Just by looking at it, you can tell it cannot support the weight of the average adult." However, if you have prior knowledge the rickety old chair is really a well-built steel chair made to look like a rickety old chair, then your faith in the chair would be strong; whereas a person who did not know about its hidden strength would think only a fool would sit in it.

The preaching of the cross is to those who perish so

much foolishness. To us who are saved, however, it is the power of God. We see more than an instrument of ancient capital punishment; we see the instrument of God's salvation. Through revelation knowledge, we who are redeemed glory in the spectacle, the scandal, of Calvary, throwing our whole weight upon its power and provision.

The preaching of the cross is foolish to the unregenerate, but preaching itself is foolish to the secular mind and carnal heart. Preaching has fallen upon hard times in many areas of modern culture. The reason is quite clear. The goal of much preaching is not in line with divine purpose; thus, it is not effective. The best fork in the drawer is no match for the ugliest spoon if you want to eat soup.

Preaching by itself is becoming less and less relevant because preaching is being used for human goals: to help people be more successful in a temporal world, feel better about themselves, make the sinner comfortable around Christians, educate people in biblical morality, present a Christian worldview, make Jesus an add-on to a non-Christian lifestyle.

If the American pulpit would begin to see preaching as a tool of the Holy Spirit, it would be incredible how relevant it would become again. When preaching results in transformed lives, restored families, healed bodies, and broken habits, people's faith will again stand upon God's power and not human wisdom.

Showing Faith in What God Can Do

Paul approached his ministry with fear and trembling because he did not want people to put their faith in what he could do but in what God could do. His was the same attitude expressed by Peter and John after the man at the Beautiful Gate was healed: "It is Jesus' name and the faith that comes through him that has given this complete healing to him, as you can all see" (Acts 3:16).

The "edge" in Pentecostal preaching is total dependence on the power of the Holy Spirit. That edge is lost when preachers decide their primary role is to help but not heal, counsel but not cure—when they prepare their heads with a message but not their faith for the miraculous.

It is a mistake for Pentecostal preachers to point back to the early days of the past century as their model for ministry. It is imperative they look back to apostolic days and emulate their message and faith. The power of apostolic ministry was preaching and demonstrating Christ. When they looked at the mission of their ministry, they echoed their Lord, "With God all things are possible" (Matthew 19:26).

Paul shows the Pentecostal preacher how to use education, eloquence, wisdom, and all the acquired skills of ministry. He makes it clear God can use learning and human ability, but the preacher cannot depend upon any of it to make a difference without the power of the Holy Spirit.

The challenge of the pulpit in twenty-first-century America is to be in the center of divine activity and to preach a faith centered on the crucified and risen Christ with signs and wonders following. Too many preachers are satisfied with doing their best and glorying in their abilities and past accomplishments. By so doing, they preach themselves and what they can produce. This results in people putting their trust in the messenger, not the message.

Undermining the Power

A misplaced faith touches every aspect of the church. It is sad to monitor many pulpit committees seeking a pastor. The résumés include accomplishments such as church growth under the candidates' leadership—as it should. The committee seeks information on the candidates' education—as it should. However, few committees inquire about the supernatural results of the candidates' preaching, their prayer life, and their ability to lead people to Christ. Such a pattern leads to human appointments instead of the will of God.

The profile of the minister in contemporary

Pentecost must be changed to reflect the significance of the pulpit, the focal point of ordained ministry. From the pulpit, the written Word is proclaimed in such a way that the living Word can be demonstrated.

All kinds of things, good and not so good, are undermining the preaching of Christ in the power of the Spirit. Pulpit time is often shortened to accommodate singing and worship teams. Special days and programs displace the preaching of the Word entirely. All of this tells the American church that preaching is not the centerpiece and priority of the worship experience.

Preparation time for the pulpit is also being eroded. The troubled seek relief by making appointments with the pastor who has become a good counselor. The result is a transfer of faith by the people from the power of God to the expertise of their pastor. They no longer expect great things through pulpit ministry. If these pastors are not careful, they will begin to think they are obligated to meet the expectations of people at the cost of their divine obligations.

Paul speaks powerfully to the contemporary preacher and pastor. By his exhortation and example, he urges study and excellence, yet places the burden to do the impossible upon the Holy Spirit, "struggling with all his energy, which so powerfully works in me" (Colossians 1:29). Paul brings focus to the primary message (Jesus Christ and Him crucified). And he gives hope to every ordained minister because what he accomplished he did through the same power that is resident in every Spirit-filled believer and gospel preacher.

Our forefathers are often criticized for their dim view of education and lack of balance in preaching grace. But it would not be surprising to discover a great majority of their congregations, despite their foibles, believed God to do the impossible and testified to supernatural deliverance. Would it not be marvelous if twenty-first-century Pentecostal ministers were well-educated and well-prepared but upon coming to the pulpit would say, "I come to you today in fear and trembling, without eloquent words of human wisdom, but I come with a word from the Lord and with an expectation that God will demonstrate His power."

Adaptable Without Compromise

Paul was a great Pentecostal preacher because he was adaptable to different cultures, connecting with a variety of audiences without compromising the integrity of the gospel message. He was a renowned preacher to the Jewish community of believers; at the same time, he was called to be an apostle to the gentiles. A point of tension with his Jewish brethren, an impossible task in the natural, nevertheless, Paul's ministry would not be limited by culture or demographics.

Because Paul was effective in cross-cultural situations, both inside and outside the church, a great deal can be learned from him for ministering in America. Because of his ability to be flexible in temporal issues, his adamant stand on eternal truth was enhanced. He did not turn people off by insensitivity.

Between Absolutes and Culture

Paul knew the difference between eternal absolutes and cultural tradition. He fought for the eternal but was very flexible with the temporal. A great example of his insight and wisdom involved the controversy over circumcision. In the opening verses of Acts 15, Paul confronts Jewish believers who were teaching that a man could not be saved unless he was circumcised according to the Mosaic tradition. The problem became so critical that a council was held in Jerusalem to address the matter. Paul withstood all of the arguments, insisting that the Church no longer teach the doctrine of circumcision as necessary to salvation.

Given Paul's strong stand at the Jerusalem Council, one would think he would insist that no male ever be circumcised again. Yet in the very next chapter of Acts (16), Luke records his insisting that Timothy be circumcised "because of the Jews who lived in that area" (v.3). Was Paul compromising his message of grace? Not at all. At the Jerusalem Council, the argument involving circumcision centered upon salvation. The situation with Timothy had nothing to do with salvation. Although his mother was "a Jewess and a believer," his father was a Greek. It was a cultural barrier which needed to be removed in order for the gospel to be preached. Paul was never willing to adapt the message of the cross and the risen Christ, but he was willing to adapt himself and those who ministered with him—"so that by all possible means I might save some" (1 Corinthians 9:22).

Romans 14:14 reveals one of the underlying principles of Paul's ministry: "As one who is in the Lord Jesus, I am fully convinced that no food is unclean in itself. But if anyone regards something as unclean, then for him it is unclean." His view of things by themselves was amoral. How he used things was determined by how they affected others. Free of legalism, Paul was nevertheless bound by love. The practical application of this principle is vital to Pentecostal preaching. In the recent past, the Pentecostal pulpit leaned toward identifying certain things and activities as evil in themselves. Young people were turned off by harsh statements such as, "If you are in a movie theater when Jesus comes, you will be left behind." Broad interpretations of friendship with the world or being unequally yoked meant isolation from everyone but Pentecostals, including a total ban on involvement in sports.

Paul would not have consigned anyone to hell for eating certain foods, especially after Jesus had "declared all foods 'clean'" (Mark 7:19). "Why should my freedom," Paul asked, "be judged by another's conscience?" (1 Corinthians 10:29). In his time, food offered to idols was a debatable item; in our day, it would be going to a theater or a dance. Paul would preach a message of responsible behavior within the context of an agape fellowship. If going to dances or a theater offended spiritual leaders because of their concern for young Christians or new believers, Paul would have put aside any personal involvement for the sake of unity and edification. He would have preached the restraint of love, not legalism.

Lest one think Paul was a compromiser, condoning sinful and worldly practices, one need only to look at his stern warnings and clear preaching against sinful behavior leading to spiritual death. Paul was quite clear there were sins against God's law, such as adultery, rebellion, character assassination, homosexual activities, and lying, which destroy a person's relationship with God for time and eternity.

The preacher of today confronts a complex, dualistic, tolerant, relativistic society; it is a changing culture that challenges the absolute truth of God. Paul's life and teaching give the Pentecostal believer and preacher the guidance needed to discern what is eternal and temporal, wise and unwise, good and evil.

Addressing Various Audiences

Not only was Paul adaptable to changing culture, but he was also able to speak with clarity to a wide variety of people groups. This ability should come as no surprise since the very essence of Pentecost broadened the entire concept of the Church. Where once the Jews believed they alone were God's chosen, Jesus redefined the category as "true worshippers" (John 4:23). Where once the place of worship was confined and God had a temple for His people, after Pentecost, God had a people for His temple. Where once the Hebrew tongue was the tongue of religion, after Pentecost, all tongues expressed the glory of God.

Paul recognized the need for the pulpit to speak to every people group. His missionary travels took him into countries and before audiences not only resistant to new truth but also suspicious of any Jew, to say nothing of one who preached such a radical message. Of course, Paul did not always meet with success and was almost killed on several occasions, but the record of churches he established and the number of miracles he performed on these journeys are quite remarkable.

Spirit-filled missionaries of today have learned how

powerful and adaptable the message of Christ can be to all nations. The dimension of Pentecost that makes the gospel effective in all cultures needs to be emphasized in modern America. Through the power of the Holy Spirit, the truly effective pulpit can find a way to transcend racial prejudices, language barriers, and ethnic cultures. America's Pentecostal preachers must believe that the Holy Spirit can make them effective in reaching and discipling the growing mix of nationalities at the doorstep of their churches.

Paul's ability to touch all nationalities goes back to his single focus. Wherever he went in the world, he preached Jesus. He did not preach a Jewish culture or personal opinions. After the church was established, Paul led the new believers into the process of indoctrination and the culture of the kingdom.

Whenever and wherever missionaries have followed the Pauline model and preached Jesus, the response has been gratifying. However, when an "Americanized" gospel has been preached and an "American church" has been established in foreign countries, the result has always been limited growth at best and total failure in most cases.

The modern students of religion are telling the contemporary church what Paul the apostle knew: "Religion turns people off, especially a culturally oriented religion; but Jesus appeals to every kind of person." The logic is unassailable. If Jesus is the answer to evangelism and church growth in any timeframe or culture and if the Holy Spirit was sent to reveal Jesus, then the only effective ministry in the cultural diversity of modern America is a preacher ordained of God and filled with the power of the Holy Spirit with a Christ-centered message.

Chapter 6

The Pauline Model— Part Two

Besides being certain of his call, having a Christ-centered focus, demonstrating power in his ministry, and being adaptable without compromise, Paul had more traits to recommend himself to the twenty-first-century minister.

Exercised Godly Wisdom

Because sin has so darkened the thinking of the worldling, the result is the antithesis of wisdom, namely, a foolish heart, inevitably producing a fool (Romans 1:21-22). At the same time, there is a rare natural wisdom in the world today. At all levels of society there seem to be those unusual people who instinctively apply knowledge with sanity. The Spirit-filled preacher, however, must meet a higher standard. In 1 Corinthians 2:4, the apostle wants the church to know he did not come to them with "wise and persuasive words" of the world. Thankfully, he no longer came to the church with "murderous threats" (Acts 9:1) either; he now spoke "a message of wisdom among the mature" (1 Corinthians 2:6), a wisdom "from heaven" (James 3:17). Paul was a great Pentecostal preacher because he exercised godly wisdom.

The Limits of Human Wisdom

The minister must understand that human wisdom falls far short of the wisdom needed to operate within

God's kingdom. No matter how wise a person may appear to be, the wisdom for ministering to and through the church is beyond the ability to acquire on one's own. That is the very reason the apostles chose men "full of the Spirit and wisdom" (Acts 6:3) to minister to the needs of widows. They realized that in the church something as ordinary as serving tables involved relationships that called for spiritual insight. It is a mistake for leaders in Pentecostal churches to hire or appoint experts in a certain field if these experts are spiritually deficient. In the kingdom, a treasurer needs to be filled with the Holy Spirit as much as a pastor. A janitor needs the touch of God as much as a deacon.

It is not difficult to imagine that from time to time Paul exercised the Spirit's gift of the word of wisdom to edify the body of Christ. But his wisdom was not limited to an occasional manifestation. It was a state of being, a part of his makeup as a Spirit-filled believer.

Paul came out of a religion based upon pride of tradition and superior wisdom. When he came into the Pentecostal faith, he viewed human wisdom as more of a barrier than a blessing. His fear was that the "wise" person would look at the cross of Christ and declare its message to be foolish, rejecting God's plan of salvation and making it "of no effect" (1 Corinthians 1:17, NKJV).

Paul knew better than anyone else how inherently deceitful human wisdom could become. As a matter of fact, he gives a warning in the most direct manner and proceeds to offer a cure: "Do not deceive your-selves. If any one of you thinks he is wise by the standards of this age, he should become a 'fool' so that he may become wise" (1 Corinthians 3:18). The Pentecostal preacher is not immune to this self-deception. Human wisdom is tempting. But by giving in to the temptation to seek human wisdom as a first priority, the higher wisdom of the kingdom is missed.

The Principle of Preparation

From the very beginning of Paul's ministry, he revealed a superior wisdom every preacher should seek.

After having experienced a spectacular conversion, how tempting it would have been to offer a sensational testimony to increase influence and ministry. In Paul's case, he was also highly educated, had exhibited obvious leadership abilities, and he was given a divine mandate as an apostle to the Gentiles. At the same time, the churches were under great stress and desperately needed a man like him. Besides, what a temptation to "get on with it." But no . . . he would not appeal to all this as giving him a right to assume leadership.

Paul makes a reference to a three-year period between his conversion and a visit to Jerusalem (Galatians 1:18), a period that has been the basis of a great deal of speculation. We do know he went to Arabia, where it seems reasonable to assume he took a significant amount of time for reflection. There in Arabia, perhaps in the vicinity of where God delivered the Law, Paul prepared himself to preach the fulfillment of that Law and to fully accept the word of the Lord through Ananias: "I will show him how much he must suffer for my name" (Acts 9:16).

Bypassing preparation and study is unwise for those called of God. Christ himself who knew His life would be short did not enter public life until He was 30 years of age. Those who point to the apostles as uneducated men overlook the fact they were tutored for three and a half years by the greatest "professor of theology" in the history of religion. Those who are called to the Pentecostal ministry should know that the greater the task, the greater the preparation—and there is no greater task on earth than the responsibilities inherent in the ordained ministry. Paul warned Timothy, for example, about the dangers of promoting a novice: "He must not be a recent convert, or he may become conceited and fall under the same judgment as the devil" (1 Timothy 3:6). Allow me the privilege of emphasizing again: the greater the task, the greater the preparation.

In the long view, those who took years of study and training had greater spiritual results and crowns to place at the Master's feet. Throughout 40 years of ministry I have observed the results of those who took the time to complete a good educational program and those who scoffed at ministerial training. Almost without exception, the latter group had ineffective (and more often short-lived) ministries. Great harm has been done to the Pentecostal Church by those who, once anointed to the kingly task of the ministry, bypassed obscurity and began looking for giants to kill. David killed Goliath after facing down lions and bears. If people are ordained to preach, God will promote them to office; but until He does, the duty of His anointed is to accept years of preparation right where they are. The greatest calling in the kingdom is servanthood, not leadership (you cannot demote a servant). The ultimate job of a servant is to obey, not command.

The Principle of Priorities

Closely aligned to the principle of preparation is the principle of priorities. Everything Paul did was centered on the work of the kingdom. As already pointed out, he was never "off message." In addition, he was never "off ministry." His whole passion was to make Christ his priority. This passion not only propelled him but also ruled his life. He could instinctively prioritize the activities of his life.

When Jesus said, "No servant can serve two masters" (Luke 16:13), He was pointing out a situation both impossible and unwise. Serving two masters is impossible in the sense you cannot please two ruling authorities; they will be in conflict. A person may appear to serve two masters, but when the test comes, one master will have to take precedence over the other. Serving one master is a full-time job. Trying to accommodate two is both futile and foolish.

Paul was wise in his ministry because he chose Christ as his ruling authority. "Forgetting what is behind" (Philippians 3:13), he did not let his past rule him; nor did he let people control him. When believers pled with him not to go to Jerusalem, he refused to be dissuaded (Acts 20:22; 21:4,12). Anything or anyone—

no matter how well-meaning—that would have made him disobedient to the heavenly vision was seen as an attempt to reorder his priorities.

It is unwise for Pentecostal ministers to become involved in activities or situations that simply by taking time undermine the quality of their ministry. The word "take" is not a neutral term: It speaks of authority. Anything that makes the minister less effective should be avoided. Paul chose to be a tent-maker because it allowed him to help the Church without becoming a burden. So when duty called, he could respond freely; tent making was not a ruling authority or a demand on his time. He always had time to do the will of God.

Circumspect in Circumstances

Paul was wise in responding to circumstances. He was not presumptuous in his faith. For instance, when he was going to be physically attacked in Damascus, he did not say, "Bring them on! The Lord will protect me!" Rather, he escaped in a basket let down over the city wall. There were times when Paul was imprisoned, beaten, and stoned because of the suddenness of an attack, but the record shows he did not invite it. Paul used wisdom in situations where his dual citizenship was an advantage. When he needed to disclose his Jewish heritage, he did; but when it was to his advantage to play the Roman citizenship card, he did that too.

In spite of Paul's ability to respond with flexibility to circumstances, he never lied or deceived people; when a truth needed to be emphasized, he emphasized it. By becoming with integrity all things to all men, he was able to win some to Christ who would never have responded otherwise. Pentecostals would do well to learn how to attract the unsaved by wise words and a good attitude rather than repelling them with unnecessary remarks.

The confrontation between Paul and the high priest Ananias (Acts 23:1-5) is an example of Paul's humility. When Ananias ordered his men to slap Paul after his opening statements, Paul called Ananias a hypocrite, not knowing who Ananias was. However, when Paul was told he had just insulted the high priest, he apologized, noting "for it is written: 'Do not speak evil about the ruler of your people'" (v.5).

Paul exhibited godly wisdom because the Spirit of God is the spirit of wisdom. It would be difficult to overemphasize the need for Pentecostal preachers to be anointed with such wisdom: to have the ability to discern inner qualities and essential relationships, to acquire an instinctive adaptation of accumulated knowledge, to exemplify an intelligent application of learning through the Holy Spirit.

Tireless in Ministry

Paul was a great Pentecostal preacher because he put much time and great effort into his ministry. He was not bashful about how hard he worked: "I have worked harder than all the other apostles, yet actually I wasn't doing it, but God working in me, to bless me" (1 Corinthians 15:10, TLB). He reaffirms his work ethic—and its goal of presenting "everyone perfect in Christ"—in Colossians 1:28-29 and teaches his son in the gospel, Timothy, to give double honor to those "whose work is preaching and teaching" (1 Timothy 5:17).

Contrary to some thinking, good, anointed, effective preaching is preceded by hard work. The perception that Pentecostal preachers do not work hard at their calling grew out of a misunderstanding about their dependence upon the Holy Spirit to work in and through them. Granted, there was a school of Pentecostal preachers who felt sermon preparation was of the flesh and contrary to the true work of the Spirit; nevertheless, some of those who scorned formal disciplines were themselves great students of the Word, as well as being passionate and able defenders of it. They simply limited their scope of studies and spurned the science of preaching.

Sadly, there are some Pentecostal preachers who are just lazy. They are not students of the Word or anything else. Claiming to be dependent upon the Holy Spirit, they hope against hope He will somehow help them through each preaching assignment. Making the spurious claim what they say is the anointing, they substitute an empty head and a loud voice. For the Holy Spirit to bring anything to our remembrance, there must first be something in our heads to remember.

Paul the apostle realized that before God speaks through the preacher, He chooses to do something *in* the preacher. He worked hard and labored in the Word; and as he did, the Holy Spirit gave him the ability to preach and teach that Word. "This [preaching] is my work, and I can do it only because Christ's mighty energy is at work within me" (Colossians 1:29, TLB).

Most preachers of the Word testify to the labor that goes into an effective presentation of the gospel. An intense exercise, it requires great concentration; at the same time, one has the awareness of the Spirit's insight and guidance. The process can be likened to an apprentice and a master. The apprentice works hard but cannot take credit for the ultimate product because the master has been there to give oversight and direction. Paul recognized his responsibility but made it clear he could not meet the divine standards without the Master's input.

Paul's instruction to Timothy about laboring in the Word is most helpful: "Study to show thyself approved unto God, a workman that needeth not to be ashamed, rightly dividing the word of truth" (2 Timothy 2:15, KJV). Every word is filled with meaning and guidance, not for Timothy alone but for every preacher of the gospel. Paul sets before Timothy the challenge and the motivation to study. By inference, Paul is making a very serious charge: A preacher cannot please God and have His approval without study in the Word with the single purpose of obeying Him. Preachers are always tempted to study to gain human approval. If they yield to that temptation, however, they will study the wrong things and be satisfied with the wrong results.

The Scripture warns the minister to avoid being "menpleasers" (Ephesians 6:6, KJV). All preachers know when their goal is to please people. Sometimes the results are gratifying, but when the adulation ceases, overwhelming emptiness takes over. The preacher realizes he has not first sought the approval of the only One who counts.

Both preparing to preach and preaching for the purpose of pleasing God is the ultimate joy of the ministry. Paul wanted Timothy to experience the fulfillment that comes from obeying God rather than people. He instructed him to avoid tailoring or diluting his message to appease a congregation who wanted to hear something that pleased them rather than hearing what they needed to hear for the welfare of their souls.

Paul wanted Timothy to study hard to avoid needless embarrassment before both God and people. It should sober the minister to realize a sermon can be a disgrace in the eyes of the congregation, to say nothing of his God. The antidote to that miserable possibility is to teach God's truth correctly. The only way to do that is to give oneself continually to arduous, fervent prayer and study. The alternative is to preach other people's sermons, presume the Spirit will bless laziness, and hope no one with a greater Bible knowledge will call one's hand on a false application of Scripture.

It is an awesome responsibility to be a preacher of the Word, especially in a culture that rejects absolute truth and is even critical of opinion. The minister at this time in American history faces a population which, down deep in their souls, has a hunger for the truth but a mindset to reject it. The only solution is an authoritative declaration of the Word in the power of the Spirit. This is a result of a well-prepared heart and mind, which, though it can be challenged by the enemy, cannot be refuted or defeated by him.

Mentor of Others

Paul was a great Pentecostal preacher because he was a great mentor and encourager of other ministers.

This ability grew out of a sense of security in God and his call. Because of these, he was protected from fearing the success of others and the misunderstandings of his peers. His strength in this area is illustrated by his response to those who opposed him and took delight in his imprisonment. He was in no way defensive. To the contrary, he said, "What does it matter? The important thing is that in every way, whether from false motives or true, Christ is preached. And because of this I rejoice" (Philippians 1:18).

Giving Himself Away

The fact Paul was not defensive but secure in his ministry allowed him to give his life away and invest in others. How blessed Timothy was to have a minister like Paul to take him under his wing and train him as a true practitioner of faith and Pentecostal ministry. Paul probably picked up on this practice from Christ himself, who trained and encouraged His disciples to follow Him so they could succeed Him in building the Church. Every Spirit-filled pastor should have the goal of reproducing his ministry in the lives of young men and women.

Traditionally, the Pentecostal Church was known for the encouraging, mentoring, and training of younger ministers by older men and women. Mentoring a new generation of Pentecostal leaders is extremely critical today. For all intents and purposes, this generation is fatherless in the majority, and statistics bear out the tragic results of children without fathers. More than three-quarters of the prison population come from fatherless homes.

Paul realized how important being a father to young preachers was and is: "For though you might have ten thousand instructors in Christ, yet you do not have many fathers; for in Christ Jesus I have begotten you through the gospel" (1 Corinthians 4:15, NKJV). Instructors have an important role in ministry development, but pity the young preacher who never had a spiritual "dad" who took him under his wing and spoke the truth in love as only a father can do.

Being a Role Model

The Apostle was also a powerful role model for Timothy and other ministers. Just think of Paul's prayer life. His prayers are wonderful examples of love for God and compassion for others. The references to prayer in his writings are so numerous that to comment on all of them would require a lengthy book. Any associate of Paul's would see in him a man of prayer. Day and night he would seek God for the welfare of the churches. The greatest legacy the Pentecostal minister could leave a new generation is a legacy of prayer.

The Apostle was a powerful role model within the context of Pentecostal ministry. He was unashamed of speaking in tongues; to the contrary, he let it be known that he spoke in tongues more than anyone in the Corinthian church (1 Corinthians 14:18). His faith in exercising spiritual gifts is numerous—from healing the sick to casting out devils and even to raising the dead. His Pentecostal doctrine and practice was extremely important to him.

The Apostle was a powerful role model of compassion for the lost. Paul is viewed as a great intellect and teacher (which he was), but he was also a great evangelist and soul winner. Romans 9:3 gives a glimpse of Paul's pathos and love for souls: "I could wish that I myself were cursed and cut off from Christ for the sake of my brothers, those of my own race." The printed texts of his preaching reveal a fervent evangelist who had no greater thrill than to preach Jesus as the Savior of the lost, Redeemer of the world.

The Apostle was a powerful role model of planting new churches. In all of his travels, he sought to establish local churches, realizing that all the evangelistic fervor with signs and wonders would be wasted if new believers did not come together as a body for the exercise of the ministry gifts. The nature of Pentecost in its dimension of signs and wonders often attracts immature Christians who could be defined as seekers of the sensational; nevertheless, mature church leaders know the biblical pattern for the church is local in its function and stability. In a day of rapid travel and high-speed technology, the contemporary believer needs to understand there is no substitute for the local church and faithful commitment to and involvement in it. Paul's teaching in Ephesians 4:11-14 makes clear a believer cannot be perfected without the ministry gifts, which can be provided with consistency only in a local church. Although the Scriptures refer repeatedly to the greater body of Christ, the physical expression of the "universal" church is local. There was a church in Jerusalem, Antioch, Ephesus, et al.

Paul was a great role model in building good relationships. There is a tendency to see the confrontational side of Paul, that aspect of him that would not compromise on the great issues of the faith or the philosophies of the world. However, Paul had an ability to maintain good communication and warm fellowship with individuals and churches. He did not burn his bridges when it came to relationships. The well-known dispute with Barnabas about John Mark, with Paul refusing to take him on a missionary journey, would have severed a relationship with a prideful person. However, Paul allowed John Mark to prove himself, later inviting him to be part of his ministry. Paul's sincere greetings to churches and individuals in his letters attest to his being a true "people person," one who knew how to keep relationships in good repair.

The Apostle was a powerful role model in adversity. Every minister of the gospel can study the life of Paul and learn how a true Christian faces trouble. His chains never imprisoned his spirit. His beatings never changed his commitment to the gospel. Prisons brought out the best in him, not the worst. Even the prospect of physical death did not fill him with dread but with anticipation of heaven and eternal rewards.

A Minister of Integrity

Paul was a great Pentecostal preacher because of his integrity. No doubt there are critics of Paul today who accuse him of being legalistic in his life and teachings. However, like Peter observed, "His letters contain some things that are hard to understand, which ignorant and unstable people distort, as they do the other Scriptures, to their own destruction" (2 Peter 3:16). Besides being adamant about obtaining salvation by grace, he was adamant about the believer not being free to sin. In Paul's mind, believers were to be holy because they were saved, not to obtain salvation. Good works and righteousness were the fruit of grace. The cross was the centerpiece of humanity's relationship with God. The cross made it possible for a person to deal with sin through divine righteousness. (Christ became "sin for us.") The reason for the Lord's Supper was not only to remember Christ's death but also to examine one's heart and put away sin. The idea of a believer's justifying sin because of grace was repugnant to Paul: "Shall we go on sinning so that grace may increase? By no means!" (Romans 6:1-2)

Paul's standard of conduct for the believer was very high. His rebuke of the church at Corinth was filled with righteous indignation. He could not fathom a Pentecostal church allowing immorality to go unchecked among its members and so explained clearly how to deal with sexual sin in the fellowship (1 Corinthians 5).

Paul's teaching extended to matters of law within the body. After all, he pointed out, someday believers will judge the world. Matters of injustice between believers should be dealt with in the boundaries of biblical and spiritual principles in order to maintain the divine integrity of the Christian community.

The Apostle believed the elders of the church were worthy of double honor, but he also believed the minister should be held to a very high standard of personal conduct and integrity. The qualifications for leadership demanded a clean record outside the church and a stellar reputation within the body.

Paul took an uncompromising and, to some, radical view of holiness in his personal life. He testified to the fact there could be no compromise or ambiguity about his relationship to sin. He went through an intentional process daily of dying to self (1 Corinthians 15:31), and he admonished every believer to "count yourselves dead to sin but alive to God in Christ Jesus. Therefore do not let sin reign in your mortal body so that you obey its evil desires" (Romans 6:11-12).

Paul's fear of becoming "disqualified" (1 Corinthians 9:27) after having preached the gospel himself has certainly become warranted in our day. The public exposure of some well-known Pentecostal preachers who disgraced themselves, their Lord, and the church bears sorry witness of that all too recurrent tragedy. Everyone should realize by now that the key to holiness is more than simply believing it and preaching it. One must live it as well, including the body in a strict mental and spiritual discipline.

If the Pentecostal culture begins to embrace the philosophy of tolerance for sin and the Pentecostal ministry begins to relax itself on sin in the ministerium, the modern Pentecostal movement will begin to fade into the pages of history. Paul's lifestyle was not old-fashioned; it was eternal. Holiness, righteousness, and integrity will never be outdated, because they are in the character of the eternal God—part of the spiritual DNA of all God's children.

The life of the apostle Paul is one of the most exemplary in Scripture. We may discern self-confessed weakness and human inadequacy, but there is no record, no sign, not even a suspicion, of willful sin against God. May every Pentecostal preacher set a goal of leaving the same legacy.

A Person of Courage

Paul was a great Pentecostal preacher because of his courage. Courage has always been a hallmark of the Pentecostal pulpit. The apostles were known as powerful preachers who spoke the word of God with boldness. Actually, when confronted with a mandate to cease and desist from proclaiming the gospel they prayed for boldness (Acts 4:29), and according to

Luke's account of the incident, God forthwith answered their prayer.

The record of the twentieth-century Pentecostal church is one of great courage both in and out of the pulpit. It was common to hold meetings in the open air and in tents, on the street and in parks, where Pentecostals were subjected to egg throwing and verbal abuse. These courageous "soldiers of the cross" pressed on, and through their efforts thousands were saved and many strong churches were established.

Once, my father was preaching a tent meeting in New England with the goal of establishing a church. But when the power of God fell, neighbors called the sheriff to put a stop to the noise. While my father was still preaching, the sheriff showed up to shut down the meeting. However, when he started down the center aisle, my father felt the boldness of the Holy Spirit and shouted, "Who is on the Lord's side?" The entire crowd stood as one person. The sheriff stopped in his tracks, turned around, and walked out.

The Apostle exemplified courage among his peers. He does not appear to display any ambition to gain office or prestige within the church structure. His boldness did not stem from pride but from a clear understanding of objective truth and doctrine. He had such a command of Scripture that his arguments and logic were irrefutable by godly people. The famous confrontation between Paul and Peter over circumcision is a classic example of two respected leaders who approached a controversy from different reference points. Peter did not want to offend the Jewish believers. Only God knows if his motives were born out of fear or love of his brethren. In any event, his philosophy of accommodation was wrong and would have led to a spiritual dead end.

Why did Paul win the argument and save the day for the Church in his confrontation with Peter? Peter was probably more respected at that time than Paul. Paul was a newcomer; Peter was one of the Twelve. Furthermore, Peter was the first leader to reach out to the Gentiles, taking the message of Pentecost to

Cornelius's household. It had represented a radical departure in the life of the young Jewish Church. Then Peter seemed to reverse himself and decide to champion the Jewish believers and their tradition. At that point, Paul courageously took on the "Big Fisherman," the deeply revered and highly respected apostle Peter, and proceeded to win the argument, settling the matter once and for all. Though "a Hebrew of Hebrews," Paul was the champion of Scripture and theology, not tradition.

Jesus was crucified because of His courage in the face of militant religious tradition. If He had taken the position of compromise, or even accommodation, to attract the scribes and Pharisees and "bring them along" in such a way as not to offend them, we would not have had a Savior and we would still be in our sins. This same result is possible today in the congregation that sits at the foot of a Pentecostal pulpit that promotes accommodation—no conviction, no Savior, and still in their sin.

To sustain and build the true Church of Jesus Christ today, it is going to take the courage of Paul, based as it was upon an absolute faith in the gospel of Christ. Paul was willing to be as flexible as anyone when it came to nonessentials, but if anyone toyed with the integrity of Scripture and the grace of God as revealed in Christ, he was like a lion—a true defender of the faith.

Paul was also courageous in facing the world system and its enemies of the Church. He was not ashamed of the gospel or any part of it. He did not hesitate to point a finger at the Jewish community of Jerusalem and declare them guilty of crucifying Christ. He was not afraid to address the polytheistic intelligentsia of Athens and proclaim monotheism. He was not afraid of Rome and the political might of Caesar. As a matter of fact, he knew his defense of the gospel would result in death there. Nevertheless, he faced that prospect with divine calmness and peace.

And "by faith he still speaks, even though he is dead" (Hebrews 11:4). In a day when voices within the church tell the preacher to avoid offending the outsider with the message of the cross and the blood, Paul answers: "May I never boast except in the cross of our Lord Jesus Christ" (Galatians 6:14). In a day when the world demands tolerance of sin, Paul says: "Do not conform any longer to the pattern of this world" (Romans 12:2). In a day when the church and the world want the preacher to avoid being dogmatic, Paul says: "The grace of God that brings salvation . . . teaches us to say 'No' to ungodliness and worldly passions" (Titus 2:11,12). In a day when the world says it is arrogant for a person to declare absolute truth, Paul says: "I know whom I have believed" (2 Timothy 1:12).

Let the Pentecostal Church be the center of Bible truth. May her pulpits declare without equivocation the whole counsel of God. May her preachers once again warn of a hell to shun and gladly teach there is a heaven to gain. May Christ be preached with Holy Spirit boldness and scriptural authority. In a day when the American Church is feeling pressures within and without, all Pentecostal preachers would do well to make Paul the hero of their faith. The preaching of Paul and people like him has proven to be the method God has ordained to save people from their sins. No other gospel! No other name!

A Love for Christ

Because of his love for Christ, Paul was a great Pentecostal preacher. Everything he did was motivated by an insatiable desire to please God (Colossians 1:10) and to possess Christ in fullness (Philippians 3:8). He counted everything not related to pleasing Christ as a waste of time, an entry in the debit column.

Paul's love for Christ should surprise no one. The ministry of the Holy Spirit is to reveal Christ and testify of Him. It follows that if someone is filled with the Spirit, he or she will be completely possessed with a desire to know Christ and serve Him. Paul's love for Christ gave meaning and balance to his message and ministry, as it should to every believer and minister of the gospel. Love determined the value and significance of everything. Because Jesus Christ was the most significant and valuable relationship in Paul's life, everything and everybody were judged in relation to Christ.

Because Paul loved Christ, he loved humanity, especially that part of the person most valuable to God—the eternal soul. This love sent God's only Son to die in everyone's place so each individual could have eternal life. This same love motivated Paul to endure all the hardships the world could inflict upon him (and they were considerable). This is the love that should create and sustain a love for souls in the heart of every true preacher of the gospel.

Paul's love for Christ gave him a deep and abiding passion to build the Church, the earthly expression of the Lord's body. Those whose actions say they do not love the Church are in effect saying they do not love Christ. If a person died to bring something into existence, how one treated that something would prove one's love for the person who brought it into existence. A traitor will sell out his country to the enemy; a champion will defend it with his life. These analogies hold true for allegiance to the Church of Jesus Christ.

Paul's love for Christ gave him great patience, respect, and appreciation for his peers. The fact that Paul was a powerful bishop and apostle is often emphasized, but his dependence upon and submission to the church council at Jerusalem is often overlooked. He was no self-important guru who decided he had achieved such an "enlightened" position he did not need the advice and direction of his brethren. Consider his missionary journeys, begun with the first missionary sending agency in the history of the Christian Church. Though driven with a deep desire to "Go into all the world," he did not answer only to God; he also conferred with church leaders, who prayed and concurred with the affirmation of the Spirit. Then he and Barnabas went out with their blessing. Paul had an exalted title within the church, but his greatness did not come from his title but from his spirit of humility, cooperation, and love.

Paul reminds every believer of the "more excellent way" (1 Corinthians 12:31, KJV), that the greatest of all gifts to the Church is a passionate love for Christ. From this vital relationship flows a transcendent power, which makes up for human weakness and limitations. Even the most inarticulate can be eloquent when inspired by love. Paul's love for Christ gave him patience with Timothy and his companions, wisdom to diffuse the most volatile situations, and an abiding peace in the face of death.

The Pentecostal church has been known for its desire for the supernatural and the operation of all the gifts of the Spirit, but all of it is to no avail if the most gifted of preachers drive people from God and the church. In times of uncertainty, inside as well as outside the church, the power of love for Christ infuses confidence, steadiness. It is also the source of moral safety in an immoral society. Without it, power corrupts and fanaticism is a germ that multiplies in its absence, but "love [abounds] still more and more in real knowledge and all discernment" (Philippians 1:9, NASB).

Paul's life and letters testify to all of us that God's love never fails; we need try nothing else. Let all Pentecostal preachers determine to be their very best, never forgetting that love is the one quality which makes all other disciplines and gifts meaningful and effective.

Chapter 7
The Pentecostal Preacher

The minister who speaks in tongues approaches ministry in a distinctive manner from those who do not. Of course, the work of the Spirit in the preacher who has not spoken in tongues is wonderful and profound, but the work of the Spirit in and through a Pentecostal preacher can and should have a powerful, supernatural dimension.

Paul the apostle certainly discovered the value of tongues in his life as a preacher. With deep gratitude in his heart, he wrote: "I thank God that I speak in tongues more than all of you" (1 Corinthians 14:18). He goes on to correct a misuse of tongues in the Corinthian church, but his joy in exercising the gift of tongues is evident. Since God does not show favoritism and the Pentecostal baptism is promised to every believer as a family gift, that is, the gift of the Father, every preacher—aware of needing all the help that's available—would do well to lay aside all fear and receive this divine provision.

The gift of tongues is to be exercised both in private and in public. Sadly, Paul's need to give instruction to the Corinthian church in the proper use of the gift has been used by sincere evangelicals as a reason to do away with the gift altogether. The entire debate over tongues is most unfortunate. In most cases, it has led to a diminishing of spiritual power in the personal and public life of the preacher.

Paul instructs the Corinthians to insist upon an

interpretation of tongues in public because the use of tongues is to edify the church through supernatural utterance; thus, an interpretation of tongues is necessary in order for the congregation to understand what was said supernaturally. Paul had no desire or intent to do away with public tongues. He simply wanted them to be exercised in a proper manner.

When Paul admonished the church to seek the gift of prophecy in contrast to the gift of tongues, he was pleading for the church not to neglect other gifts. The Corinthians had so focused on tongues they had neglected prophecy. However, Paul does remind the church tongues with interpretation is equal to prophecy (1 Corinthians 14:5).

Those critical of tongues often point to Paul's dissertation on love in 1 Corinthians as "the better way" to do ministry but fail to point out 1 Corinthians 14:1: "Follow the way of love and eagerly desire spiritual gifts." It is not a case of either-or but both-and: both spiritual gifts and love.

The argument that spiritual gifts ceased at the end of the apostles' ministries has been greatly muted by the millions who have received the baptism of the Spirit with the evidence of tongues, and thousands have gone on to use spiritual gifts with great effectiveness. The gifts of God are obviously scriptural and available and active today.

The initial experience of being baptized in the Holy Spirit with the evidence of tongues is just that—an initial experience. It is the proof of God's ability to take complete control of an individual through the Spirit's power. However, more important is being continually filled with the Spirit as a lifestyle. This can be accomplished only by submitting to the Spirit and allowing Him to have complete control day by day.

The Spirit-filled preacher has the right and privilege to be controlled and directed by the Spirit in every aspect of his life and ministry. The implications of this fact are staggering. His thought life is controlled by the Spirit; his prayer life, family life, and church life are all guided by the Spirit. His preaching and ministry can all be done in the power of the Spirit, not in degrees but in fullness. The fact many who claim to be Pentecostal but do not obey the command to walk and live in the Spirit does not take anything away from the availability of the Spirit and the desire of Christ for His ministers to be endued with supernatural power from on high.

The meaning of being Spirit-filled is to be controlled at the core of the will. When Paul said he went to Jerusalem "compelled by the Spirit" (Acts 20:22), he was confessing to the power of another who compelled and directed him in much the same way men were "moved" by the Spirit as they penned the Holy Scriptures. Why then are people who claim to be Spirit-filled not infallible? Because unlike evil spirits, the Spirit of God controls only the will of the person He inhabits. The work of the Spirit can be gauged in people's lives in direct proportion to allowing the Spirit to control their will. The apostle Paul admitted to a battle between the flesh and the Spirit in his life. Doubtless there were times when the flesh won (cf. Acts 15:39; 23:3).

The daily goal of every Pentecostal minister should be the same goal of every believer, that is, to be daily filled or controlled by the Spirit of God. That goal can be met only by first dying daily to oneself and then being renewed inwardly through the work of the Spirit. When a person does not intentionally die to self by slaying the ego, the carnal life is allowed to renew itself and dominate the will. The carnal life becomes more and more obvious: selfishness, irritability, harshness, anger, unkindness, defensiveness, insecurity, stubbornness, greed, and a long list of other spiritual ills.

Unfortunately, the very nature of ministry lends itself to self-centeredness. Even in this cynical culture, preachers still command a great deal of respect. They are looked up to as teachers and guides. Their advice is sought on a vast array of issues, some of them intimate. Add to all of this the power of the pulpit, and it is easy to see the inherent danger of preachers becoming proud of their own abilities.

The antidote to pride is humility, and there is no greater way to be humbled than to compare oneself with Christ. The preacher has this ultimate question to answer: "Will my ministry be all about myself or all about Christ?" The key word is "all"—all of Christ: His mind, His love, His grace, His power, His character. That comes about only by being filled with Christ's Spirit, not with one grand visitation but by an intentional intimacy motivated by a continuous desire for Him to be formed in you all day, every day.

The proof a preacher is truly Spirit-filled and Pentecostal can be outlined in five dimensions:

Dimension One: Spirit-Filled Character

The Pentecostal preacher maintains a Spirit-filled character. Without the fruit of the Spirit, all of the other characteristics of a Pentecostal ministry are nullified and the operation of the Spirit's gifts undermined.

The fruit of the Spirit is the character of Jesus Christ spontaneously lived out through the believer who is abiding in the vine. The operative word is "spontaneously." It results not from the discipline of the human will but from the indwelling, controlling Spirit of God. When the Holy Spirit is in control, then the spirit of the individual offers no resistance to the will of God. This unquestioning obedience produces supernatural fruit, such as love, joy, and peace. The person who wills to love or be patient will have a measure of success, but it will be the fruit of human effort. The fruit of the Spirit is by definition supernatural; it is "of the Spirit."

It is by this fruit of a ministry a church is to judge their preacher's spirituality. For too long the proof of a preacher's success has been judged not by character but by natural or acquired giftedness and the number of people attracted to the church. This criteria has caused untold confusion and sorrow in the body of Christ. Why God allows preachers to perform miracles and operate in the realm of the supernatural while living a double life is known only to Him. But this dichotomy is not only known to Him; in eternity it will also be judged by Him. Those who would point to mighty works and miracles done in the Lord's name as giving them the right to enter heaven will have a rude awakening. "Away from me, all you evildoers," God will thunder. "I don't know you" (Luke 13:27).

Perhaps part of the answer to iniquitous miracle workers is the Lord's desire to have His people not to focus on those things that can lead to deception. In the last days, the Anti-Christ will use the supernatural to perform mighty miracles. If people judge the validity of a minister by his ability to do great works in God's name, they set themselves up for accepting the Anti-Christ as the true Christ.

Signs and wonders can easily deceive people; however, when people have the courage to examine a wonder-worker's character, they either expose a false ministry or validate a Spirit-filled one. For a time, a false shepherd can deceive brilliantly even when judged by the fruit of the Spirit; but as people really get to know a pastor/teacher, true character will be exposed. When things do not go their way, false preachers will reveal the fruit of carnality. They will not love those who do them wrong. They will lose their temper, becoming impatient with good people, grab for everything they can get to better themselves, demand to be served, and heap sarcasm and seek petty revenge on those they do not agree with. That is one of the reasons the Lord wants His people to know those who exercise spiritual authority among them (Hebrews 13:17).

The Holy Spirit is by definition the Spirit of holiness. Pentecostal preachers who are filled with the Spirit will be of sterling character—wholesome, principled—wherever they are encountered. It will always be safe to follow their lead because they are close to God. Nothing dirty or unclean will come out of their mouths, whether at home, in church, or in the company of sinners. They have a good name because they always keep their word, meet their obligations, and tell the truth.

Let the test of a twenty-first century Pentecostal ministry be the test of character. May the introduction of anyone in ministry be, "He is a good man, full of the Holy Spirit. Incidentally, he is a brilliant preacher," or "Incidentally, he often exercises the gifts of faith, miracles, and healing," or "Incidentally, he is an incredible musician." Without a Spirit-filled character, any minister—no matter how gifted or charismatic—is doomed.

Dimension Two: A Spirit-Filled Mind

The Pentecostal preacher has a Spirit-filled mind. This vital dimension is often overlooked, especially in the areas of sermon preparation and delivery.

The Lord promised His disciples that when the Holy Spirit was outpoured, He would guide them into all truth. An intriguing question logically follows. How will the servant of God be guided into truth? It would seem the Scriptures alone would be the source of truth and their careful study the only reliable resource of truth for the preacher. There are some who believe any dependence upon any other source for truth is not only dangerous but also forbidden.

The statement "No one can say, 'Jesus is Lord,' except by the Holy Spirit" (1Corinthians 12:3) should shock all preachers of the gospel into realizing how dependent they must be on the Spirit's work in the realm of absolute truth. Of course, anyone can say "Jesus is Lord," but no one can say "Jesus is Lord" with revelation truth without the Spirit; and without that revelation, preachers will misrepresent Jesus to their audience. Jesus will be known only as a historical figure or what the best thinkers and theologians think He is.

Jesus was very concerned about His disciples knowing who He was by what God revealed to them, not by what others thought of Him. He asked them, "Who do people say the Son of Man is?" (Matthew 16:13). They told him that some thought He was Elijah or Jeremiah or one of the prophets. Jesus was not surprised that the carnal mind would speculate about His identity. His real concern was with those who would represent Him after Pentecost. One can almost see His piercing eyes when He asked, "Who do you say I am?" (Matthew 16:15). Jesus knew if His disciples did not know him through revelation, He would be presented to the coming generations as just another prophet or a great teacher. Peter, the most impulsive and unschooled disciple, was seized by a revelation from heaven. Could it be he saw the real Jesus in fact for the first time? "You are the Christ, the Son of the living God" (Matthew 16:16). Jesus answered: "This was not revealed to you by man, but by my Father in heaven" (Matthew 16:17). The Lord was stating clearly Peter had learned how to receive revelational truth through a spiritually oriented mind.

In sermon preparation, the Holy Spirit is more than a powerful resource. He brings life to dead words. The dictum "The letter kills, but the Spirit gives life" (2 Corinthians 3:6) is an ageless principle. Of all people, the Pentecostal minister should know its implications. There is a tendency to put too much weight upon the letter itself and not the meaning behind the letter or, if you will, the spiritual dimension in the context for truth. The Spirit-filled mind sees truth from a divine point of view. Earthly knowledge and wisdom are not the context to understand or proclaim divine revelation. The truth of God can be understood only through the lens of the Spirit. "The man without the Spirit does not accept the things that come from the Spirit of God" (1 Corinthians 2:14).

Apollo 13 narrowly missed disaster. A mishap on board the spacecraft jeopardized the lives of the crew. The captain radioed Mission Control and said simply, "Houston, we have a problem." To those who followed U.S. space exploration, those understated, matter-of-fact words had a chilling effect. To someone who paid little attention to the space program and was unaware of Apollo 13, those words would have sounded routine: "Officer, could you tell me where Elm Street is?" The statement "Houston, we have a problem" outside the context of our space program could lead to all kinds of conjecture and faulty interpretations. The same can be said of those who try to interpret Scripture outside the context of a Spirit-filled mind.

Those who teach hermeneutics and homiletics should do so with the utmost care. They should explain the value of these subjects. At the same time, they should point out how limited they are (as with any other subject, for that matter) without reliance upon the Holy Spirit to illuminate the mind.

Above all, the Spirit-filled mind will be in self-analysis with the mind of Christ. The Spirit will constantly remind preachers that their role is that of a servant, not of a lord or ruler over God's heritage. High-handed preachers are a danger to their flocks—flocks put under their care by the Lord. A true shepherd is willing to lay down his life for his sheep; he knows his role from the perspective of the mind of Christ.

Dimension Three: Spirit-Filled Communication with God

The Pentecostal preacher enjoys Spirit-filled communication with God. The gift of tongues in the life of Pentecostal believers should be one of the most treasured, divine resources to be exercised day by day. If that is true of believers, it is doubly true of preachers. Their need for intimate communication with God is obvious, to say the least.

The Pentecostal preacher needs divine edification for spiritual well-being. No one is subjected to as much spiritual warfare. The ministry is a target for the enemies of the soul and the Church. This was brought home to me some years ago when I learned the Church of Satan in San Francisco set aside days of fasting and prayer to the devil. The purpose of their petitions? To destroy evangelical pastors and their families through demon power. The spirit of the age can overwhelm the mind and soul of a preacher.

Furthermore, one of the disorders of twentieth-century ministry being carried into this new century is burnout. Perhaps a new term should be introduced, namely, "burn in." Paul pointed out that the person "who speaks in a tongue edifies himself" (1 Corinthians 14:4). This is a way for Pentecostal preachers to renew their inner being. God's Spirit is not only an internal presence and a glorious feeling, He is also a burning fire, a blazing passion—a supernatural, overcoming power. If the Holy Spirit is burning within, there will never be burnout. May the fire of God burn in every preacher of the gospel!

Added to all the blessings and edification of the Spirit is the gift of a constant intimate communion between the believer and the Lord. The Spirit is not without the ability to speak to His people. If conversation is a two-way street—and it is—then the Spirit-filled preacher has an unparalleled resource.

Every preacher can testify to the frustration of not knowing how to pray, especially when preparing a sermon to address congregational needs. In order to convey the living quality of God's Word, they know that the Spirit of truth must affect their own hearts and minds.

In some ways, the preparation of the preacher can be likened to the preparation of trial lawyers. They will diligently study the law. More importantly, they will seek to discover everything germane to the case. However, they realize that simply spouting the letter of the law is not enough. They must consider the judge and the jury before whom they will appear. They must sharpen their instincts to take advantage of unknown elements that may surface during the trial. It is a well-known fact in legal circles that cases are won in chambers; lawyers know their cases must be prepared and tried in the judge's chambers in order to be successful in his court.

The preacher does much more than spout the letter of the law. A good preacher knows the sermon's power and effectiveness come more in the preparation than at the moment of delivery. Because this is so, the preacher must go beyond the words in the book and seek the mind of the truth; one's thought processes must not be limited to human understanding. The diligent preacher taps into the transcendent genius of God. How is this done? Through Spirit-filled communication with God.

When believers use their prayer language, a wonderful thing happens. The Spirit prays through them and for them. Paul said he prayed with his understanding but he also prayed in the Spirit, beyond the ability of his understanding (1 Corinthians 14:15). "In the same way, the Spirit helps us in our weakness. We do not know what we ought to pray for, but the Spirit himself intercedes for us with groans that words cannot express" (Romans 8:26). This scripture crystallizes our understanding in these matters: The Spirit's work in prayer commences when our ability fails. The passage concludes with this powerful statement: "And he who searches our hearts knows the mind of the Spirit, because the Spirit intercedes for the saints in accordance with God's will" (Romans 8:27).

Likewise, the preacher approaching the task of conveying truth can be reassured by the Spirit's armaments, among them, spiritual communication by which the Spirit himself intercedes. This results in an uncluttered mind and an open channel through which God can pour truth through supernatural revelation.

No preacher in the twenty-first century should try to operate as a communicator of truth without the fullness of the Spirit and all of the divine enablements available to the minister of the gospel. The gift of tongues expressed through prayer is of inestimable value because it gives the preacher the ability to speak to heaven in the Spirit and through the Spirit. Additionally, he is given the ability to hear from heaven through the instrumentality of the Spirit. "He who has an ear, let him hear what the Spirit says to the churches" (Revelation 2:11).

Dimension Four: Spirit-Filled Direction

The Pentecostal preacher is given Spirit-filled direction. The Spirit's promise to guide us into all truth is not limited to one or two functions. It seems obvious that if a person is under the total control of the Spirit, he or she will constantly be given direction in all circumstances.

The New Testament church and its leaders were successful in turning their world upside down because they were always dependent upon the Holy Spirit for His direction and were humble enough to be obedient when the Spirit spoke.

When the church began to grow, its leaders were given guidance for setting the church in order with deacons full of the Holy Spirit and wisdom. The great missions enterprise was launched when the Holy Spirit spoke and commanded Barnabas and Saul to be taken out of a local setting and sent out to preach the Word in Selucia, Cyprus, Salamis, Papas, and other cities and countries. In addition, Barsabbas and Silas were sent by direction of the Holy Spirit to the Gentiles. The ministry of the Holy Spirit in guidance and direction is a reality throughout the New Testament.

The Pentecostal movement has been marked by supernatural guidance and direction. The opening of new mission fields around the world are the result, in most cases, of people being thrust forth by the Spirit. The country of Brazil was opened to the Pentecostal faith by two preachers from Sweden who were told to board a ship and get off at the first Brazilian port and start a church.

In the earliest days of the Pentecostal revival in America, young people would be called to foreign lands, in some cases to cities they had never heard of. Obeying God's call, they went, some of them packing their clothes in caskets because they knew they would not return. Millions of people are in the kingdom of God because hundreds of missionaries were supernaturally directed to their homelands by the Spirit.

It would not be surprising to learn that a majority of Pentecostal churches were started by preachers seized by an overwhelming compulsion to leave a comfortable situation and begin a new church in a new city.

Bethel Church of San Jose, California, a large and thriving Pentecostal church, was started by a preacher named E. O. Roebeck in 1947. He was pastoring a good church in Southern California only to be directed by the Holy Spirit to sell everything, move to San Jose, buy a piece of property, and start constructing a church by himself. Knowing this was supernatural direction, he did just that. One day as he was shoveling dirt to put footings in place, a Pentecostal contractor stopped by and asked what he was doing. Unbeknown to either of them, the contractor was to help build the church—both physically and spiritually—becoming the first deacon in a God-directed and God-ordained church plant. The annals of Pentecostal history are filled with these kinds of stories.

The Pentecostal preacher is not only given physical direction, but he is also given supernatural direction in the preaching and conducting of public services. Nearly every Pentecostal preacher can tell of incidents when the Spirit of God told him to change the order of a service and form a healing line or appeal to the lost to come to the altar or give a word of exhortation outside the context of the sermon.

C. M. Ward, the great evangelist, was leading an altar call and, for some strange reason, had the musicians sing "In the Garden" several times. "In the Garden" is a beautiful song, but it does not suggest itself as being appropriate for an altar call. However, a man who had resisted the call of God broke under the conviction of the Holy Spirit and came running to the altar. Later it was learned that "In the Garden" was the favorite hymn of his godly mother who had prayed for his salvation for many years before her death.

Dimension Five: Expectant of Signs and Wonders

Pentecostal preachers can and should expect signs and wonders to be part of their ministries. This emphasis should be woven throughout the fabric of a Pentecostal ministry. From the opening pages of the New Testament to the last, the Word is full of preaching and teaching on the supernatural. If ministers of the gospel want to present themselves as New Testament preachers, their message will include a heavy emphasis upon a miracle-working Jesus. They will believe that if Jesus is alive, then the days of miracles are not past.

The miraculous starts by preaching faith. There is an old truism that needs to be heeded (if not repeated): "You get what you preach." Paul understood this well. He realized believing something was not enough; he had to proclaim it. Pentecostal faith must be preached and demonstrated. Proclamation of truth should always lead to the demonstration of that truth. The Word of faith must always be followed by the works of faith, or the proclamation becomes a theory, not a reality. The Day of Pentecost was marked by a supernatural outpouring of conviction resulting in 3,000 turning to God. This account is soon followed by the story of Peter and John going to a prayer meeting and on their way healing a lame man through their faith in the Jesus they declared.

The days of miracles are not past for those who believe, proclaim, and practice supernatural faith. But for those who choose to believe differently, the days of miracles are past. Those who are hungry for the Word of God to go forth in the demonstration and power of the Spirit will be rewarded for their faith.

Pentecostal preachers are doubly blessed to be ministering in the twenty-first century. Not only do they have the joy of preaching a resurrected and ascended Christ, but they also have the privilege of experiencing and proclaiming the person and work of the Holy Spirit within the context of the prophetic word. Our God has declared "no good thing does he withhold from those whose walk is blameless" (Psalm 84:11). Can anyone imagine our Lord giving the Holy Spirit with the evidence of other tongues, which He calls the gift of the Father, to one person and then withholding it from another? Can anyone believe the Lord of the Church would perform miracles through some preachers and withhold that blessing from others? Can anyone conceive of the Holy Spirit ministering His mighty anointing through one denomination and not another? Pentecostal preachers in the twenty-first century can have all the resources of the Holy Spirit at their disposal with all of the attending signs, wonders, and miracles.

Chapter 8

The Pentecostal Leader

Jesus promised His disciples He would build His Church. He did not promise to build their church, nor did He say they would build His Church. Translated into practical terms, if the Lord is not building, guiding, and directing a church, then people are trying to do so; and they labor in vain. The result is a human religious organization—which will produce what people can produce and will last as long as people live to perpetuate what people have created.

Pentecostal preachers do not proclaim truth in a vacuum. They do not present humanistic philosophy; they deliver the Word of the Lord in the power of the Holy Spirit. They are not just proclaimers, but under God they are also builders. Granted, they are builders of people, but they do so by building on foundational truth. The sermon is a divine building block, not an isolated function or order of service.

Just as the sermon needs to be understood in context, so the preacher's role must also be seen in the same way. The minister is a preacher, but he must preach from the perspective of being a leader—a builder. Ephesians 4:11-12 speaks to the fact that ministry gifts (ministers) are in place to bring people to perfection so they in turn can function as God's church in the world. The believer is a "portable temple" who, in the truest sense of the word, is the church individually when the church is not meeting corporately.

Total Dependence on God

The Pentecostal preacher as a leader in the New Testament was distinguished by total dependence upon God the Father, the preeminence of Christ, and the person and work of the Holy Spirit. The catalyst for that dependence was prayer. Prayer was and is the means whereby the Lord of the Church communicates His will to His "subcontractors." The written Word is the grand design, the eternal blueprint, which includes a manual for church builders as well as the desired character and discipline of the workers. However, the Lord is not building a physical, temporal building. He is building a living, growing, developing organism. Yet to be completed, His Church is not a finished product. He is still at work; we are still in process.

The builders of the New Testament church were able to read the plans by studying the written Word, but they also knew the Spirit had to bring the Word to life and guide them in applying truth to unique and contemporary situations.

The Founder of the Church, Jesus, set the code for every building of the Church. It can be expressed in three words: "dependence on God." He proved His dependence on the Father by His prayer life. It should humble every minister to hear these words of Jesus: "By myself I can do nothing" (John 5:30) and "not my will, but yours be done" (Luke 22:42). It was He who taught us to pray, "Your will be done on earth as it is in heaven" (Matthew 6:10). The only ways to know the will of God are to read His Word and to hear His voice. The only way to hear is to listen. The only way to listen is via prayer. If the sinless Christ—God in the flesh—felt the need to pray constantly to start the Church, how vain to think that those whom He ordained to the work of building the Church can do so without prayer.

An Occupational Hazard

The occupational hazard for any Pentecostal pastor or minister is to become dependent upon human wisdom as the source of effectiveness. How tempting to transfer faith from the intangible, the unseen, to those methods others have used with great success. This surrender to temptation is followed by prayerless study and carnal application. However, here is a divine mystery: Those who are not dependent upon human methods are free to use them—with this rider: "under the direction of the Holy Spirit."

The temptation to simply copy a success is almost overpowering, but copy cats are not leaders. There is a way to resist that temptation, however: Draw inspiration and faith from success but believe God for greater works. Jesus taught that anyone who had faith in Him would do "even greater things" than He himself did because He was "going to the Father" (John 14:12). He was telling His disciples He did not want them to copy His works but to be guided by the Holy Spirit He would send to them after His ascension. Many human efforts have failed because they were spent on trying to reproduce in the flesh what God alone can do through the Spirit.

Travel the Pentecostal world and you will find every conceivable church polity, methodology, organization, and administration. Leadership models and methods in the Pentecostal world today are as varied and unique as the people using them. Those who seek the single biblical model for church governance will be sorely disappointed and confused to the point of frustration.

Pentecost is spiritual life and power, not carefully structured and maintained church government. Different means are used to bring natural power into church buildings. There are different kinds of wiring, plumbing, generators, and so on, but the mechanics are lifeless until power flows through them. In the same way, there is need for human channels, sharp minds, and articulate spokesmen; but all of them are dependent upon the flow of the Holy Spirit to bring spiritual life and power. They are truly effective in building the kingdom only when the Holy Spirit is allowed to guide the ministry. For the Bible warns about the possibility of "having a form of godliness but denying its power" (2 Timothy 3:5).

There is no definitive governance structure in the Scriptures because God knew church leadership would become more concerned about getting structures and titles right than trusting the Holy Spirit to perform the ministry of Christ.

Pentecostal leadership must maintain primary dependence upon the Holy Spirit, or they will become dependent upon non-Pentecostal methods and produce non-Pentecostal churches. The danger is in dependence. It is a temptation to lean upon the arm of flesh. There are some well-packaged religious programs on the market, but there is no substitute for seeking the Lord and depending upon Him to build His Church through human instrumentality. There are no turnkey ministries in the kingdom. Any idea or program must be tailor-made or Spirit-edited to fit into the plan of God for any given situation that takes spiritual leadership.

Producing What Cannot Be Manufactured

Besides being tempted by a well-packaged religious program, the preacher can easily fall into the habit of constructing sermons and implementing programs that please people but do not change them. Preachers are faced with a clear choice: Will their preaching be for pleasing people or transforming lives? Will the programs they institute come from the leading of the Lord or the pressure of members or peers? Pentecostal ministers are primarily in the business of producing what cannot be manufactured, namely, the works of God. May they never be satisfied with temporal results and success. If they decide to seek God, knowing they cannot produce one thing of eternal value, then God will take that "foolish" message they are preaching or that new creative ministry and build His Church, confounding the world.

The principle of dependence on God must be the bedrock of the Pentecostal preacher in or out of the pulpit. Many church bodies have been diminished by pastors who depend upon God as preachers but not as leaders in the administration and operation of the church.

The Early Church reveals a group of Pentecostal leaders who saw themselves guiding congregations through uncharted waters. Because of this fact, they sought God for every detail involving their churches; they took nothing for granted. The results were supernatural. Twenty-first-century churches face the same challenges as first-century churches: Contemporary church leaders also must guide their congregations through uncharted waters. Only God knows what lies ahead. Today's leaders must protect themselves from being deceived. Just because they have become knowledgeable about successful church models and principles of administration does not mean they know how to apply such knowledge. For example, leaders can learn how to conduct a business meeting, but they cannot know how God wants to use such a meeting unless they are led by the Holy Spirit.

There is no set way to "do" church, the right way to preach a sermon. There is either God's way or man's way. Be reminded: "So are [God's] ways higher than your ways" (Isaiah 55:9). The uniqueness of Pentecostal leadership is found in its faith and trust in God, not in a predictable routine, process, or methodology. God uses foolish things, weak things, to confound the mighty.

An Unhealthy Dependence

One of the dangers facing the Pentecostal church is the unhealthy dependence upon secular, professional expertise. The unhealthy factor inserts itself when leaders substitute research for prayer and make human advice determinative. This modus operandi is seen more and more in the process of filling the office of senior pastor. Instead of the churches being called to fasting and prayer, as was the norm in recent Pentecostal history, pulpit committees are increasingly turning to profiles, résumés, and educational criteria, with only lip service to prayer.

Would a pure New Testament Pentecostal ministry model automatically exclude human specialization and secular expertise? Most certainly not. The Early Church used buildings, contemporary transportation, wisdom, and common sense in sending out missionary teams and establishing routines of prayer, study, and fellowship; and they took advantage of education.

The contrast between a healthy (biblical) and an unhealthy (secular) model of church building can be clearly seen in the way leaders determine the role human instrumentality and professionalism will play in decision making. The Pentecostal leader will seek the will of God first; then, led by the Spirit, he will use or add human expertise to fulfill the divine vision and goal. The carnal Pentecostal will seek human counsel first and then expect God to put His blessing upon what has already been determined.

The true Pentecostal church was and is still being built by leaders who often defy human wisdom, put the most unlikely people in the most unlikely places, plant churches without human resources, laugh at impossibilities, and live by faith based upon unseen evidence.

The true Pentecostal preacher-leader not only maintains a dependency upon the Holy Spirit but also finds ultimate security through his relationship with Christ. The law of cause and effect is at work in the process: The person who depends upon the guidance of the Spirit will find a divine security in Christ because the mission of the Spirit is to make Jesus Lord of all things, past, present, and future. The opposite is also true: The preacher who does not depend upon the Holy Spirit will depend upon the arm of flesh—which will most certainly fail.

God desires His ministers to have confidence that will give them boldness in preaching, courage in the face of opposition, peace in troubling circumstances, and clarity in a time of confusion. None of these characteristics can be found in an insecure preacher because his security is based upon the approval of people; and as anyone knows who has been in the ministry for any length of time, nothing is more unstable and subject to change without notice than the approval ratings of a preacher of the gospel.

The Example of Paul

No greater example of a true minister-leader can be found than the apostle Paul. Over and over, his boast was in Christ, starting with his salvation in this life and ending with his deep conviction that death was better yet because it would mean unbroken fellowship with Christ forever. Paul's security in Christ overcame every apprehension that might stem from criticism.

The Spirit of God had borne witness with Paul's spirit that he belonged to God. That knowledge of his place in God led to the immortal words: "I am convinced that neither death nor life, neither angels nor demons, neither the present nor the future, nor any powers, neither height nor depth, nor anything else in all creation, will be able to separate us from the love of God that is in Christ Jesus our Lord" (Romans 8:38-39). Any preacher who is not in Christ is in trouble.

The frantic search by preachers for exalted titles such as "apostle" or "prophet" is most disturbing; it reveals a diminishing and even negative attitude toward servanthood. Paul gloried in his role as a servant of Jesus Christ and used other titles only to describe various roles of ministry. The apostle Paul was bivocational: He was a servant-apostle, a servant-leader, a servant-bishop. His strength was in his servanthood, not his apostleship.

The greatest leaders in Pentecost were not marked so much by great preaching as they were by great service. The founders of the modern Pentecostal movement were men and women who were secure enough in their relationship with God that they did not need to protect their positions. They preached on street corners and in rescue missions and storefronts until God

provided church buildings. They prayed with people—
sometimes for hours—until victory came. They left
home and family and went to unknown tribes in foreign lands without expecting to return. The power of
the Pentecostal church has always been in service, not
in human ability.

One of the hallmarks of Pentecostal leadership has
been a total disregard for the opinions and demands
of ungodly people and carnal Christians. The disciples'
message set the collective teeth of the religious
hierarchy on edge; they had them beaten and ordered
their message stopped. The reaction of those disciples
revealed their strong convictions and courage. Instead
of worrying about the consequences of a tribunal's
wrath, they focused on the will of the Master and
counted it a privilege to suffer for Him.

Twentieth-century Pentecostal preaching, especially
in the first 75 years, was focused on eternity and the
condition of the soul. Accused of being legalistic
and full of "hellfire and brimstone" preaching, they
nevertheless had great results in reaching the lost
and creating a culture of holiness.

It could be argued men and women who visited a
Pentecostal church in the 1940s and 1950s stood a
better chance of confronting sin, trusting in the blood
of Christ for salvation, maintaining a healthy fear of
eternal judgment, and longing for heaven than in the
mainstream American Pentecostal church of today.
The insecure Pentecostal preacher is a threat to those
who sit under his ministry because he will invariably
preach from the paradigm of what will please people
or self rather than "This is what the Lord says." A
leader full of the Spirit, secure in Christ, and
confident of his calling is a powerful gift to a lost
world or a confused believer. He will preach the whole
truth and nothing but the truth in the fear of God and
out of love for eternal souls. He will not be a follower
of people but a leader under God.

Because of Paul's dependency upon the Holy Spirit,
he was secure in his leadership. He was secure

enough to want the finest and best to work with him. Proof of this fact is clearly illustrated by his treatment of John Mark. At first, he honestly felt John Mark was not right or ready for the mission field. Later, he saw the development and growth of John Mark and requested that he join his team. In making such a request, Paul shows his own maturity, having changed his mind about John Mark; and in accepting the invitation, John Mark shows great humility after experiencing a traumatic rejection.

The Early Church sought out and commissioned good men full of the Holy Spirit to join leadership in moving the church forward under God. And the apostles exhibited no fear or jealousy toward those, such as Stephen, who rose to prominence among them. Similarly, contemporary Pentecostal leaders show their security when they want to surround themselves with the most spiritual and qualified people available. Because these leaders' security is in Christ, they have no fear of losing their ministries. On the other hand, any insecure leader will be threatened by those who are perceived as better preachers or teachers than themselves.

Persecution

Because of Paul's dependency upon the Holy Spirit, he was secure in the midst of great trouble and persecution. If the faith of the Early Church leaders had not been solidly in the resurrected Christ, they would have quickly succumbed to the unrelenting pressures of their world. But a hostile religious community and corrupt government seemed to have strengthened their resolve and their courage to preach an uncompromising message. Of course, such strength came from a daily infilling of the Holy Spirit. Of a truth, wrote John, "The one who is in you is greater than the one who is in the world" (1 John 4:4).

Persecution is nothing new to the Pentecostal community. Some middle-aged Pentecostals can remember their fathers losing their jobs because of their faith;

church buildings were often damaged or destroyed. Pentecostal children suffered abuse from their peers and were consistently labeled "holy rollers."

American Pentecostals had a reprieve from overt persecution for a number of years near the end of the twentieth century. But a more aggressive persecution is about to come against the true Church of Jesus Christ in America. For example, to many politicians, homosexuality is no longer a moral issue; it is a civil rights issue. This shift is ominous. Legislation will be put in place to make preaching against homosexual activity a hate crime. Preachers will have to mute their message or face fines. Modern culture is going to become increasingly demonic and hostile to the church. Only leaders who are secure in Christ will be able to stand.

Consequently, twenty-first century Pentecostal leaders will need the constant infilling of the Spirit to be strong and uncompromising in their message and mission. Although the pressures upon them may be different from the pressures of the past, they are pressures nevertheless. And spiritual warfare remains intense. Persecution is more subtle, but it is still a reality. Spiritual leaders in America are not jailed, beaten, and stoned—true. However, they are under pressure—both inside and outside the church community—to soften their message, to be tolerant of sin, and to seek consensus instead of staying true to their convictions.

In addition to dependence on the Holy Spirit and security in Christ, the true Pentecostal preacher-leader will find his effectiveness in the power of God. Paul's declaration should be said in conviction by every Pentecostal preacher: "My message and my preaching were not with wise and persuasive words, but with a demonstration of the Spirit's power, so that your faith might not rest on men's wisdom, but on God's power" (1 Corinthians 2:4-5).

Early-twentieth-century Pentecostals have been roundly criticized by more "enlightened" students of that era. However, criticism should be constructive and not destructive. It should be a tool for improvement in methodology and greater effectiveness in fulfilling mission as well as strengthening core values. Modern criticism within the American Pentecostal community has proved to be more destructive than constructive for several reasons.

Legalism

One of the most strident attacks against early Pentecostals occurred in the area of legalism. Without a doubt, some of the preaching of this era bordered on the absurd, and in some cases undermined justification by faith and the grace of God. At the same time, many preachers were sincerely concerned about holiness and sanctification. Though defective in their emphasis upon appearance and behavior, they believed firmly that justification by faith and the grace of God made it possible to lead a holy life.

Though early Pentecostals may have tended toward legalism, there was no problem of alcoholism in the body. When fornication took place, it was not ignored when discovered. Divorce was almost unknown, even as the world began to accept it. There was a deep loyalty to the church; attendance at church was more important than school or work.

Pentecostals need to ask this question: "Has the criticism of our fathers led to a more truly sanctified and holy community of believers?" If it has not, our criticism has been more destructive than constructive. In other words, it is always easier to tear something down than to build something better.

One also has to wonder if the fear of legalism has been allowed to overcome the fear of God, resulting in a dereliction of duty by some spiritual leaders. In a day when the world rejects all absolutes and the church has provided very few standards for lifestyle and behavior, the Pentecostal leader must restore an emphasis on biblical holiness and sanctification.

The power of God is the result of a holy relationship with Him. To use power contrary to the one who grants it is to defeat the purpose of having that power, rather like a kingdom being divided against itself. Our Pentecostal forebears' emphasis upon holiness and sanctification grew out of a strong desire to be instruments of God's power. They knew the destructiveness of sin in any relationship, especially with a holy God. A new generation of Pentecostals must maintain the goal of their spiritual parents and encourage a holy people who love God more than the world and hate sin more than they desire human approval. The Lord still says, "Be holy, because I am holy" (1 Peter 1:16).

It would be naïve to think our Pentecostal forebears were not adversely affected by the world. One of the glaring examples of this reality was a very wide acceptance of racism and a clear resistance to reconciliation. To a great extent the evil of racism is being dealt with for what it is by more and more Pentecostal leaders, and very encouraging efforts are being made to heal the sins of yesterday.

While Pentecostal leaders of the past preached a strong message of holiness, they failed to recognize that the holiness of God demands a pure relationship with all people, including all races. Their reasoning for practicing segregation was rational from a worldview, but patently unscriptural. It is important to honor our elders in the faith, not to worship them but to learn from them.

Psychology

Another attack upon early Pentecostal leaders came because of their disregard for seeking and understanding the causes of psychological problems. Counseling as a separate function of the pastor's role was unknown. Any kind of mental or behavioral disorder was dealt with at the altar and in the prayer room. "Praying through" was more the emphasis than "talking it through." Results were mixed. Many were left frustrated by deep, unresolved problems when Pentecostal pastors and friends would say, "Just pray about it." At the same time, others came face-to-face with the fact that many psychological problems find their roots in sins of the heart and the mind. In the presence of Spirit-filled people at an altar, troubled people confronted their sin, repented before God and His people, and were gloriously delivered.

One has to ask the question, "Is the emphasis upon education in the behavioral sciences and counseling in Pentecostal circles resulting in greater deliverance, better relationships, and more secure believers?" Were people better off in the hands of untrained, Spirit-filled believers whose only tool was prayer, or are they better off with highly trained practitioners who rely primarily upon human insight and the tools education provides? The answer is obvious. The ideal would be highly trained, educated Pentecostals who would rely completely upon the Holy Spirit to use their education and give godly counsel in biblical principles with fervent prayer.

When a counselor decides on helping people without a heavy emphasis on prayer and the ministry of the Holy Spirit, the results of the practice will be the same as that of any secular practitioner. The counselor who seeks God and depends upon the Holy Spirit has a distinct advantage over those who do not. God will answer with supernatural insights and divine power to set the mentally disturbed free and bring spiritual healing to fractured relationships. The effectiveness of a Pentecostal counselor, whether a pastor or a full-time practitioner, can be judged quite accurately by what place the altar is given, what role the Holy Spirit is granted, and what part education plays in the counseling process.

The Supernatural

The secret of Pentecost is the supernatural. From the initial outpouring on the Day of Pentecost to this moment, true Pentecostalism is marked by the unexplainable, the unique, and the unexpected. Take the supernatural out of Pentecost, and you have no defining element that sets it apart from any other evangelical entity.

As the twenty-first century opens, Pentecost around the world is experiencing an amazing resurgence of signs and wonders. Missionary leaders bring witness to God's power at work through the Pentecostal church. Divine healing is on the rise. Documented cases of the dead being raised to life, though uncommon, are not unknown in some countries, and demons are cast out on a regular basis in foreign crusades and churches.

The challenge facing the Pentecostal church in America is unbelief regarding the supernatural. Some criticism of early Pentecostalism in America centers on a misuse of tongues and prophecy. Others point to the moral failures of high-profile Pentecostal preachers who were strong proponents and practitioners of the miraculous. Still others point to unsubstantiated claims that could not stand either the test of time or close examination.

Despite the miscues and embarrassing claims, the mantle of the miraculous still rests on the Pentecostal church for very good reasons. It was the Pentecostal church which introduced the revival of the baptism of the Holy Spirit with the initial physical evidence of speaking with other tongues. It was the Pentecostal church where people went when they had become weary of religious routine, deadening rituals, and uninspired preaching. The Pentecostal church offered a refreshing change. No one could predict what was going to happen.

The early Pentecostal church had a lot of things going on which drew derision and warranted criticism. The flesh was certainly not quenched enough; and in many cases, the pulpit remained unnecessarily weak in the ministry of the Word. In spite of all the "spots and wrinkles" of early Pentecost, a lot of divine things happened through the faith of Spirit-filled preachers and godly people.

The history of American Pentecostalism will have many pages dedicated to the miraculous. It will include hundreds, even thousands, of accounts of drunkards staggering into missions and churches—walking out sober after a meeting with God, never to drink again. It will tell the stories of hundreds of families who came to God as a direct result of a mother or father being instantly healed of something doctors had given up on. It will tell of well-ordered services being interrupted by God's order, resulting in people standing for hours in the presence of God, worshipping, being filled with the Spirit, being called to full-time ministry and career missions. It will tell of churches on the rocks of resentment and bitterness being lifted by a wave of repentance and forgiveness.

What will fill the history of the early twenty-first-century American Pentecostal church? It is certainly God's will to endue the pulpit with power from on high. It is certainly not God's will to have a weak and compromising pulpit. It is God's will to pour out His Spirit upon all flesh with resulting signs and wonders. It is certainly not God's will to relegate the supernatural to a time and a place. It is God's will to multiply the effectiveness of a Pentecostal church through a new passion for the lost and a new faith which believes that with God all things are possible . . . even in America . . . even now. It is time for the Pentecostal preacher to take the lead into a fresh emphasis upon the supernatural.

Chapter 9

The First Pentecostal Sermon

The serious student of Pentecostal preaching should focus on outstanding examples of sermons by Pentecostal preachers. The message delivered by Peter, fresh from the Upper Room, is incomparable. It is the first sermon in which Christ is presented as the savior of the world following His ascension. The implications of this fact are enormous. In a sense, the Holy Spirit is saying to every preacher: "In the absence of a physical Christ, this is how I want you to preach. I want you to present the great themes of this message to a skeptical world with my direction and power."

God's sovereign orchestration of events on the occasion of Peter's sermon is breathtaking—in the vessel chosen and the makeup of the congregation in its ethnicity, demographics, and religion. Furthermore, the immediacy of the message following the outpouring of the Spirit adds to the importance of the event and the effectiveness of the message.

Peter's sermon was not delivered in a vacuum. Like all effective Pentecostal sermons it had a history. On the divine side, it began with God's ordination of a very unlikely candidate. Peter appears to be the last one who should have been chosen. In truth, every person called of God is inherently unworthy to assume the role of a preacher of divine truth.

On the human side, Peter's message was an outgrowth of obedience. From the day Jesus called him, Peter's life was forever changed. With all his human foibles and failures, Peter sought to follow Jesus and obey His commands. These facts are also applicable to every true servant of Jesus Christ.

Because of obedience, Peter was a preacher. Obedience was the reason he became a Pentecostal preacher. The risen Lord had commanded the 120 not to leave Jerusalem until they had been endued with power from on high. If they had not obeyed, the story of the Christian Church would have unfolded in a radically different way.

It would not stretch credulity too much to imagine that if Jesus' command to wait for the coming of the Holy Spirit had been given prior to His resurrection, Peter would have said, "Not me, Lord!" However, Peter had learned through bitter personal experience Jesus was always right about everything; so when the Lord said, "Wait until . . . ," there is no recorded argument from Peter. After Jesus' post-resurrection appearance to him, Peter had definitely become a different person.

No wise man attempts to do a great work beyond his ability without assurances from someone greater than himself. Peter had reviewed the record of his worldly ambition, contentious spirit, and cowardly behavior and knew he needed to be more than he was and possess more than he had before attempting the Great Commission. He knew that without God's power, he would be a total failure; so when Jesus offered the gift of power through the Spirit, Peter was ready to receive.

The Spirit that filled the disciples and rocked Jerusalem started a new order. The nature of the Church was changed, and a transcendent dispensation for its preachers began—transcendent in the sense of revelation, understanding, methodology, and demonstration. They were "endued with power from on high" (Luke 24:49, KJV)—not just any power, but the power that affected every part of their lives and ministry. The lessons from Peter's sermon are many and important for the Pentecostal preacher.

Never Be Ashamed

The true Pentecostal preacher should never be ashamed, embarrassed, or put off by the supernatural demonstration of the Holy Spirit. In every sense, the church on the Day of Pentecost was on fire. That fact should surprise no one since the forerunner of Christ, John the Baptist, had given fair warning: "I baptize you with water for repentance. But after me will come one who is more powerful than I, whose sandals I am not fit to carry. He will baptize you with the Holy Spirit and with fire" (Matthew 3:11).

On the Day of Pentecost onlookers were attracted by a group of people who appeared to be intoxicated—full of spirits. Of course, the onlookers misread the group's behavior, but they could see and hear something out of the ordinary had happened at the "Upper Room Church" that morning. What transpired in the city of Jerusalem on the Day of Pentecost was something unexplainable. When people came to find out what was going on, they were confronted with the supernatural. They were confounded, amazed, and in doubt because they heard something they had never experienced: a supernatural demonstration of languages that communicated the wonderful works of God. The diverse crowd understood the diverse languages, but they knew the locals did not have the ability or the background to speak them. Because the out-of-towners could not understand this demonstration, their first response was predictable: They criticized.

What if Peter had been embarrassed about the demonstration on the Day of Pentecost? What if he had said, "You know, we should have used more wisdom today in how we conducted ourselves. Discussion has already started as to whether all this emotion is warranted. Above all, we want Christ to be glorified, and we apologize for emphasizing the work and ministry of the Holy Spirit. We want you to know—if you come back to the Upper Room Church, the leadership will not allow anything like this to happen again." However,

Peter was not embarrassed; he was thrilled.

The truly effective Pentecostal ministries—from Topeka, when the first believers in the twentieth-century received the baptism, to Azusa Street and on to this moment—have not been ashamed of Pentecost. To the contrary, they have preached it, prayed for it, and given place for the manifestation of the gifts of the Spirit.

Throughout history the church ultimately became what it believed and preached. When Luther and Wesley preached salvation by faith, their churches became filled with redeemed people. When preachers began to waver on the authority of Scripture and salvation through the blood, their churches became filled with unregenerate souls. When our forefathers preached the baptism of the Holy Spirit with the evidence of tongues, divine healing, and other signs and wonders, their churches filled up with hungry people who expected and witnessed the mighty miracles of God, confounding the unbeliever. When Pentecostal preachers begin to question their own doctrine and excuse a lack of divine power, their churches soon consist of people who do the same. They are not hungry for the baptism of the Holy Spirit and do not want anything out of the ordinary to happen in church. The reason? Supernatural demonstrations are not part of their core belief because their pastor does not preach and believe for such manifestations.

Depend upon a Revelational Hermeneutic

The true Pentecostal preacher is a biblical apologist and depends upon a revelational hermeneutic. This gives him an authority that matches Peter's on the Day of Pentecost. No one else can so confidently explain the divine. No one else can say, "Listen to me. I can answer your questions about the supernatural." This should not surprise anyone, for the Spirit came to guide us into all truth.

Peter introduces his sermon with a negative, "These men are not drunk, as you suppose," and defendable logic, "It's only nine in the morning" (Acts 2:15). He confronts error and cynicism. In other words, he does not allow the skeptic to go unchallenged. The human mind instinctively attempts to explain the unexplained; however, the Pentecostal preacher will use this tendency for the purpose of expanding upon the reality of God and His works (cf. Acts 17:23). It is here the tension builds between the carnal and spiritual.

In God's kingdom there should be no conflict between the educated and the uneducated, but too often, that is the case. Peter stands before us as a type of the "unschooled" and "ordinary," yet he knows many things by the Spirit the highly educated theologian cannot learn apart from the Spirit. Higher education and hermeneutics can be and are used of God, but He is neither limited nor bound by them. Without the Spirit, Peter was often confused, superficial, and inept. Under the Spirit's influence, however, the fisherman rivaled Cicero in oratory, equaled the emperor in power, and exceeded Einstein in knowledge. When Peter correctly answered Jesus' question about His identity, Jesus pointed out such knowledge had not been revealed to him "by man, but by my Father in heaven" (Matthew 16:17-18). Smith Wigglesworth was an uneducated plumber whose wife taught him to read and whose only reading thereafter was the Bible. When he preached, however, he became, in the words of Donald Gee, "a Pentecostal phenomenon": "When preaching he became tangled in long involved sentences. Then he would relieve our perplexity by speaking angelically in tongues which he always interpreted himself. It was all part of the sermon. Explain it how you will, there were some remarkable flashes of revelation. The preacher himself probably little understood the sheer theological depth and insight of his own words."[*]

Peter, the uneducated, and Paul, the educated, were both powerful and effective Pentecostal preachers and teachers. Both of them performed mighty miracles and saw signs and wonders consistently follow their

*Colin Whittaker, *Seven Pentecostal Pioneers* (Springfield, Mo.: Gospel Publishing House, 1985), 36.

ministries. Both of them spoke with tongues. Both of them added to the canon of Scripture.

What was the commonality between Peter and Paul, the uneducated and the educated? They were both obedient servants of Jesus Christ and filled with the Holy Spirit. They did not neglect their relationship with the Lord or their total dependency upon the Spirit. Neither man neglected the highest education: an intimacy with Christ by an intimacy in the Spirit.

Higher education can be and often is a blessing to the Pentecostal pulpit. The advanced courses Paul took under the scholar Gamaliel certainly did not adversely affect his ministry. God chose Paul's highly trained, anointed mind to better explain the deeper truths of God through the written word. The reason Paul's education was not a problem is because he did not depend upon it to do what only God could do. He did not allow higher education and criticism to diminish the supernatural, deny the miraculous, cast doubt on the deity of Christ, or question the Pentecostal experience. Furthermore, Paul—like Peter—stayed true to the Word of God.

The crowd on the Day of Pentecost was stunned to hear the preacher point back to one of their prophets and verify the amazing outbreak of spiritual phenomena and power. Peter did not say, "This could be interpreted as a fulfillment of prophecy," or "I believe this is of God." He said what every Pentecostal could say when believers are filled with the Holy Spirit: "This is what was spoken by the prophet Joel" (Acts 2:16). "This is what happened on the Day of Pentecost." "This is what was promised by the Lord our God for the last days."

The Pentecostal preacher has an obligation to point confused and doubting minds to the Scripture. Peter did not emphasize human emotion; he validated the supernatural experience that caused the emotion. He acknowledged there was a great deal of emotion or he would not have commented on the behavior that looked like drunkenness. Peter confronted the same problem all Pentecostals face, namely, the desire of doubters to study human behavior rather than the fulfillment of biblical prophecy and promise.

For years, Pentecostals have faced criticism because believers get excited when they experience the infilling of the Spirit and speak with tongues. Peter had the same problem, but he handled it the way all ministers should: He appealed to the authority of Scripture. His sermon was filled with Bible references. If it had not been, he would not have had the results he did. He would simply have started an argument he could not have won.

Center the Message on a Risen Christ

The true Pentecostal preacher will ultimately center his message upon a risen, contemporary Christ. That is why the Holy Spirit was sent. Jesus said: "When the Comforter is come . . . he shall testify of me" (John 15:26, KJV). The same is true for a preacher full of the Spirit. He does not speak of himself but of Christ. A self-centered, proud Pentecostal should be looked upon as an oxymoron.

Peter, the transformed fisherman, does not wait long in his sermon to make people aware of Jesus. The apostles lived their lives in such a way the worst scoffers and enemies of the Church took note they had been with Jesus—even in the absence of a physical Jesus. They used every miracle as a reason to point the awestricken to Jesus and away from the preacher. The disciples were constantly filling their sermons and writings with the preeminence of the Son of God.

If a preacher wants to know how to present Jesus to the world, he should pay close attention to how the Holy Spirit did just that through Peter on the Day of Pentecost.

Jesus Christ—Human

First of all, Christ is presented as "Jesus of Nazareth . . . a man accredited by God to you" (Acts 2:22). The genius of the Holy Spirit introduces the humanity of Christ as a door to His divinity. This should remind us that it is just as wrong to ignore the humanity of Christ as it is His deity.

Historically, the Pentecostal pulpit has invited legitimate criticism: In this area of truth some who emphasized the deity of Christ to the exclusion of His humanity unwittingly diminished the powerful doctrine of Jesus as "a man." The preacher has the responsibility of rightly dividing the word of truth and leaving hearers with a balanced perception of Jesus as both divine and human. And when preaching on the subject of tongues, the Pentecostal preacher should never leave the perception the baptism of the Spirit is more important than the lordship of Christ.

The Holy Spirit knew on the Day of Pentecost as He does now that the limitation of the people sitting in the pew is the limitation of the preacher. He knew the congregation could not understand Jesus as divine without establishing Jesus as human. He guided the message in such a way that it led from the known (humanness) to the unknown (the resurrected God).

Jesus Christ—Divine

Peter proclaims Jesus as a man, but no ordinary man. He reminds his congregation Jesus was a miracle worker who had the approval of God. He had come from God with signs and wonders only God could do. Peter was building a case for the divinity of Christ, the ultimate revelation, which leads to eternal life. He brilliantly used the cross to bridge the chasm between God and humanity.

Pentecostal preaching personalizes the cross. It reveals to every hearer's heart the consequences of sin. The wickedness of the sinful heart was behind the crucifixion of the Son of God, the enemy's attempt to thwart the plan of salvation and leave us in our sins forever. The cross must always be the centerpiece of salvation, but the resurrection is the centerpiece of eternal life and completes the bridge between us and God. These emphases in Peter's sermon must always be in a presentation of the good news.

Note Paul in his preaching carried through the same emphasis as Peter. Paul determined to know only Christ—Christ crucified and risen again, Christ in His totality. Paul was so determined, so focused, he refused to be drawn into controversies, going so far as to have others baptize his converts for fear they might get their eyes on Paul the apostle and off Christ the Savior. Paul, like Peter, appealed to the Scriptures as his authority in preaching. "For what I received I passed on to you as of first importance: that Christ died for our sins according to the Scriptures, that he was buried, that he was raised on the third day according to the Scriptures" (1 Corinthians 15:3-4).

Jesus Christ—Relevant

The true Pentecostal sermon not only proclaims Jesus as contemporary but also makes Jesus relevant. Peter's message is proclaimed to a Jewish throng, so Peter used the fact to strengthen his thesis. He knew his congregation esteemed David, so Peter references him as a prophet of God who clearly forsaw Jesus' coming, giving details not only of the resurrection but also of Christ's struggle in hell.

The fear that the Pentecostal pulpit cannot be relevant is unfounded if it is truly a Pentecostal pulpit. The Holy Spirit will make Jesus relevant in any age or culture because the Spirit alone knows the essential, underlying, and eternal needs of humanity and presents the remedy for those needs in and through the living Christ. He does so by making the Scriptures relevant, or alive. Preachers need not concern themselves about being relevant when they proclaim Jesus in the power of the Holy Spirit.

Has someone lost the way? The Holy Spirit points to Christ and proclaims Him as "the way"!

Is someone confused about religion, not knowing what to believe? The Holy Spirit points to Christ and proclaims He is the truth!

Has someone lost the meaning of existence, finding no reason to go on living? The Holy Spirit points to Christ and proclaims He is the life!

Could it be the desire to be relevant has driven many off the message? Could it be our study of the human sciences, demographics, sociology, psychology, and even theology has convinced us our world needs another Jesus, another way, another gospel? May it not be so! To the contrary, let every preacher search the Scriptures and proclaim Jesus in the power of the Holy Spirit.

Expect Conviction of Sin

The true Pentecostal preacher will not only speak with conviction, but he will also expect those who hear his words to be convicted of sin and convinced of truth by the work of the Holy Spirit.

It is noteworthy that when Peter finished his sermon, the crowd did not feel good about themselves. To the contrary, they were "stabbed to the heart" (Williams) by the truth they had heard. Even though they were very religious and prided themselves on having most-favored-nation status with God (shades of those who feel they are all right with God because they grew up in the United States and attend a Christian church), they believed they were wicked and doomed.

The multifaceted work of the Holy Spirit includes the ministry of conviction. Jesus put it succinctly: "When he comes, he will convict the world of guilt in regard to sin and righteousness and judgment" (John 16:8).

But if one believes his natural birth created a decent person, someone who is fundamentally good, he will see no need to have a spiritual birth by God's Spirit. All the study in the world, all the arguments of logic, and all the persuasion from a pulpit can never convince nice, moral, religious people they are depraved, miserable sinners. But the Holy Spirit can.

No human being can convince another of the wrath of God and the judgment to come. The subjects of hell and the lake of fire have been missing from the American pulpit for years because the proclaimer in the pulpit has lost the revelation of people being under judgment and what they face without a saving knowledge of Jesus Christ. A deceitful universalism has muted the message of judgment. Human sentiment has displaced Scripture and declares a loving God will not send the ignorant, the decent, and the sincere to eternal torment. The preacher who has decided to proclaim human wisdom instead of God's truth is a traitor to the gospel.

When Peter preached Jesus in the power of the Spirit, the truth penetrated, moving from the head to the heart. Those who heard Peter were awakened to divine truth at the core of their being. For the first time in their lives, they heard truth proclaimed in Spirit. Because of the Spirit's revelation, they finally knew who Jesus really was.

Although the Pentecostal preacher should always know his inabilities and his limitations, he should at the same time remember the Holy Spirit's limitlessness—and lean on Him. Otherwise, he will mistake his abilities as adequate to proclaim the gospel of Christ. A sermon may convince a person he needs to convert to a certain religion, but it cannot transform a heart. The only way a person can become a child of God is to be born again by the work of the Spirit. The adage "If it looks like a duck, walks like a duck, and quacks like a duck, it's a duck" does not hold true in Christianity. That is, it is possible to look, act, and talk like a Christian yet be eternally lost.

Know How to Give an Altar Call

The true Pentecostal preacher will know how to give an altar call, or, as some would put it, "pull in the net." (The first "catch" of human souls was brought into the kingdom by a fisher of men who all his life had been a fisherman.) No one would want to go to a medical doctor who could not point to at least one patient who had been helped. No one would hire a lawyer who had never won a case in court. Success in ministry is the ability to affect souls for eternity. All the titles and trappings of religion are meaningless without eternal results.

When the response of Peter's audience told him that the work of the Spirit had been accomplished in their hearts, he took the opportunity to tell them what they should do: "Repent, and be baptized every one of you in the name of Jesus Christ for the remission of sins" (Acts 2:38, KJV). The work of the Spirit, first, brings conviction, which leads to true repentance. A hallmark of evangelistic preaching and Pentecostal meetings has been the call to the altar, or the "mourners' bench," after men and women have been convicted of their sin. In the case of the first Pentecostal sermon, three thousand people did repent and turn to God. Those who do not believe in altar calls do not serve their constituency well.

The work of the Holy Spirit at the moment of salvation is marvelous beyond description. An amazing series of miracles takes place through the ministry of the Holy Spirit: The sinner is born again and baptized into the body of Christ.

Some have misunderstood and misused the term "baptism" in the salvation experience. Peter is not speaking only of water baptism when he commands the sinner to "repent, and be baptized." He is using the term "baptism" in the sense of "being identified." When a sinner truly repents and believes on the Lord Jesus, the Spirit of God "baptizes" that person into Christ. "For by one Spirit are we all baptized [identified] into one body [identification]" (1 Corinthians 12:13, KJV). Peter exhorted the crowd to turn away from their old life of sin and identify with Christ. Only through this baptism can a soul be added to the true Church.

However, Pentecostals believe there is more than one kind of baptism. The baptism, or identification, by the Spirit at salvation is to be followed by baptism in water as an outward act that symbolizes the inward work of the Spirit in identification. Most Pentecostals reject as a serious error the teaching of baptismal regeneration. A person is baptized in water because he is saved, not because he wants to be saved.

On the Day of Pentecost the crowd outside the Upper Room had witnessed the incredible baptism of the Holy Spirit with the evidence of supernatural tongues; obviously many sincere hearts among them would want such a remarkable gift from God. Sensing that hunger, Peter holds out before them the promise the Lord makes to all believers: "And you will receive the gift of the Holy Spirit" (Acts 2:38). However, Peter puts first things first. The gift of the Father is a family gift; so before anyone can receive the gift of the Holy Spirit, they must be born again into the family of God.

At the time of the altar call, Peter exhorted the crowd "with many other words" (Acts 2:40). Most preachers would love to know all that was contained in those "many other words." We do know Peter urged the crowd to save themselves from this "perverse generation" (NKJV). Perhaps the word "perverse" finds its meaning for the modern student in a literal definition: "turned from the right way." The apostle could certainly use the same exhortation in any pulpit next Sunday morning. He would express it in such terms as: "This modern generation has a 'whatever' orientation to the right. They do not believe there is such a thing as absolutes. They do not know where they are going; they are lost. Save yourself from this kind of thinking and lifestyle."

Because of the wisdom of God, we do not have the full transcript of this first Pentecostal sermon. We are given the great eternal themes and the kind of response a Pentecostal preacher can expect. If we had needed to know more to be effective, the Holy Spirit would have provided it.

Lead to Discipleship

A true Pentecostal sermon will lead to discipleship. Acts 2:42 says it all: "And they continued . . ." (KJV). The results of the first Pentecostal sermon went beyond an experience of salvation to a transformed life—new interests, new disciplines, new lifestyles.

A return to Pentecostalism is vital in a day when the lines between the Christian and the non-Christian seem blurred. There is no doubt about the lifestyle of a New Testament Pentecostal believer and the pagan world. The new converts continued steadfastly in doctrine, prayer, Christian fellowship, Communion, giving, and church attendance. Their personal lives were examples of Christ-like holiness—so much so that they found favor with people, resulting in the Lord's adding to the church every day.

The first Pentecostal sermon bore wonderful spiritual fruit. Thousands of souls were saved, and in turn these souls were used of God to save thousands more. It is the prototype of a successful Pentecostal pulpit, namely, effective evangelism and discipleship. The conclusion is inescapable: A Pentecostal church will produce Christians and grow disciples of Jesus Christ in a never-ending cycle.

Chapter 10
Preaching on the Baptism

When Pentecostal preachers determine to preach on the baptism in the Spirit with the goal of helping people receive the gift with the initial physical evidence of speaking with other tongues, they face a myriad of perceptions, complications, and doubts. Because of these difficulties, some ministers have been hesitant to emphasize the experience. Consequently, growing numbers of people who attend Pentecostal/charismatic churches seldom, if ever, hear a message on the baptism or are rarely given an opportunity to receive in a faith-building environment. This failure of the Pentecostal pulpit has resulted in an alarming decrease in the number receiving the baptism.

Some have suggested a contributing factor to the decline: the lessening number of Sunday night services being held by Pentecostal churches. They point out that Sunday night provided an open-ended time of prayer for those seeking the baptism. Others think many pastors have defaulted to children and youth camps, expecting them to fill the gap they do not choose to fill themselves.

Regardless, the Pentecostal pastor has an obligation to systematically teach and preach on the baptism. This includes providing regular opportunities for congregants to have the joy of receiving this glorious experience surrounded by other believers. Church leaders need an intentional strategy to raise the level of importance of the Pentecostal experience, making it a high priority on the preaching calendar and insisting on quality time for people to receive. If this does not happen, in a few short years the number of Spirit-filled people will be miniscule and the term "Pentecostal" will be an empty, meaningless designation among us.

On the other hand, those preachers who decide to emphasize the Pentecostal experience, setting it forth with sound biblical exegesis and encouraging faith with biblically balanced teaching, will be rewarded. They can anticipate new spiritual life, supernatural edification, effectiveness in evangelism, and a more spiritually mature congregation.

As the preacher approaches the subject of the baptism, he should take nothing for granted. It is a constant temptation to assume listeners know much about a subject because the teacher is so familiar with it. Wisdom suggests following the example of Paul when he came to Ephesus and asked the believers, "Did you receive the Holy Spirit when you believed?" (Acts 19:2) The preacher might be shocked to hear the believers of today say, "We haven't even heard that there is a Holy Spirit in the way you are talking about it."

Creating a Hunger

How does the preacher introduce the message of Pentecost? The same way Jesus did to His disciples: as a divine promise. So the preacher should create a hunger for the gift of the Holy Spirit from the outset, telling the congregants that God has a special blessing for them. As God's children, they need to know of the "family gift" their Heavenly Father wants to give them.

After the preacher has introduced the concept of a gift, he should then present the importance and purpose of the gift—that is, this is not an ornamental gift; this is a practical gift, one that will make a difference in the recipient's life. This fact needs to be kept in focus by the preacher because so many who have experienced the gift have not used it as they should. One of the challenges facing the twenty-first century Pentecostal preacher is a wrong concept people have concerning the baptism built up by many years of neglect and misuse.

On the whole, they have not seen Spirit-filled believers living out and testifying to the blessings and effectiveness of the Spirit's power. Perhaps the single greatest reason people neglect the baptism is because they do not understand its importance in their lives. Many Pentecostals have the idea the only purposes for speaking in tongues is to be a better witness (which few have seen modeled) and to be involved in public tongues and interpretation.

The believer needs to be instructed to disregard any poor examples and encouraged to receive all God has to offer, especially this wonderful benefit.

Great emphasis needs to be placed upon the gift of tongues as a prayer language. Throughout all congregations, there are many who are in desperate need of an effective prayer life. Contemporary believers are living in very confusing times spiritually and culturally. They face conflict in the home, moral relativism in society, and mental bombardment from the enemy. There is no question the enemy has stepped up his attacks against the Church and every true believer. Thank God we have the words of the prophet Isaiah: "When the enemy shall come in like a flood, the Spirit of the LORD shall lift up a standard against him" (59:19, KJV). God never leaves His children defenseless. One of those defenses is anointed, Spirit-filled prayer.

The Pentecostal preacher knows the joy of praying in the Spirit, but many in the congregation have not been led into that Spirit-filled prayer language. Paul's observation that "anyone who speaks in a tongue [speaks] to God" (1 Corinthians 14:2) is more than a blessing for a special few; it is a necessity for all.

Preachers can create a hunger for the baptism by expounding upon the ministry of tongues in-depth. They should point out that when believers pray in the Spirit, they speak beyond human understanding. According to 1 Corinthians 14:2, they speak in mysteries. It is the Spirit praying through them, which is a mystery to people but certainly not to God; He inspires the communication.

This divine communication opens the way to a proper understanding of the promise of power: It is power through a relationship (a constant communion through union), a power conditioned in its effectiveness by the believer's humble reliance upon the person of the Holy Spirit within. The baptism makes it possible for Christ to live in us and through us by the standard set by Paul the apostle: "I have been crucified with Christ and I no longer live, but Christ lives in me. The life I live in the body, I live by faith in the Son of God" (Galatians 2:20).

To illustrate, picture a 120-pound weakling who cannot press a hundred pounds. Then imagine the greatest weightlifter in the world getting inside the weakling. All of a sudden, weakness is no longer an attribute of the slight man, but strength. What the 120-pounder could not do in his own strength, he is suddenly able to do with ease. However, it would be another's strength. All the praise or glory would go to the strong one inside the weak one. What a strong man might do physically, the Holy Spirit does spiritually and mentally. This is an aspect of John's words "the one who is in you is greater than the one who is in the world" (1 John 4:4).

By the time the preacher finishes explaining the full dimension of the Spirit's ministry in tongues and in prayer, edification, and worship, the people will not be asking, "Do we have to speak in tongues?" but rather will begin to exclaim, "We want to speak in tongues!"

Laying a Foundation

After a hunger for the baptism has been created, the minister needs to assure the people of the validity of the experience by laying a biblical foundation. Start with the promises Christ gave to His disciples before He ascended into heaven. Jesus said, "I tell you the truth [when He who is truth says that, it is wise to pay special attention to what He is about to say]: It is for your good that I am going away" (John 16:7). This is an astounding statement. Jesus is telling the disciples that He is going to send someone to them who will be such a comfort and blessing to them it will be better for them if He physically leaves the earth.

If Christ believed and taught the sending of the Comforter was more beneficial to the Church than His physical presence—as He did—it is incumbent upon the preacher to continually emphasize this "secret" of victorious Christian living and church growth. The Lord of the Church knew what was needed to build a Church that hell itself could not overpower. To that end, He commanded His disciples not to leave Jerusalem until they were endued with power from on high, followed with a directive through Peter that all followers be filled with the Spirit.

Preachers are on good theological ground to declare the baptism in the Holy Spirit with the evidence of tongues: They have the Lord's directive, the succeeding record of the promise being fulfilled, subsequent teachings on the subject, and the divine continuum through the ages. God is not the author of confusion. If He did not want us to believe in the initial physical evidence of tongues, He would not have introduced it into the life of the Church. If he had wanted tongues to cease after the apostolic age, He would have told us. Furthermore, He would have stopped giving tongues at the time of baptism, which He does even now to millions of believers.

Disciples are to be humble followers of Christ. What He commands should be obeyed. What He desires to give should be received with gratitude. When the Lord told His disciples to wait for the promise of the Father and not leave Jerusalem until they received it, they obeyed. Because they believed and obeyed Him, they—not just the 12 but 120—received what He promised.

The Day of Pentecost

The Day of Pentecost marks the Church's birth and empowerment from heaven. It is the day when believers broke away from dead religious tradition and were joined forever as a living organism. It was the day when every believer became a priest, a witness, and a partaker of supernatural blessing.

The Day of Pentecost set in motion that which was to come for the true Church until the Second Coming of Christ. Not only was the promise of God actualized, the divine pattern for every church to come was set. This Day was the start of something— not an end in itself, not a one-time event, not the possession of a particular race or religion. The glory of the Church was and is the resurrected Christ, but the enablement of the Church was and is the baptism in the Holy Spirit.

Shortly thereafter, Peter, the Jewish fisherman who had preached the first Pentecostal sermon to a Jewish audience, who had declared the Day of Pentecost as a fulfillment of Jewish prophecy, became the catalyst for another great Pentecostal event: the outpouring of the Holy Spirit upon "all flesh"—Gentile believers. Understandably, this sermon was more difficult for Peter. Salvation had been in and through the Jews, which Jesus himself had pointed out to the Samaritan woman. But the Jews had taken too much pride in their special status. Now Peter had to come to grips with the broad scope of God's promise. To his credit, he embraced the will of God and obeyed the divine summons to minister to the Gentiles.

The Upper Room experience was an initiation into the baptism in the Holy Spirit. In a sense, the outpouring at Cornelius's house confirmed the pattern and proved the promise of Joel that the Spirit would be poured out upon all flesh—including the Gentiles. The phenomenon that astounded the Jews who witnessed the coming of the Spirit upon the believers at Cornelius's house was speaking with other tongues, "the same gift as he gave us," Peter would report (Acts 11:17). These Jews were so traditional and protective of their historic exclusiveness that the evidence of God's special blessing upon others had to be conclusive. If the Jewish believers were satisfied and convinced that speaking in tongues "proved" the infilling of the Spirit, then all other believers should be convinced of its validity.

Have You Received?

Acts 19:1-6 gives a detailed account of the coming of the Spirit upon the believers at Ephesus. It clarifies a number of things for the preacher who would lead people into the truth of the Baptism.

The first question asked the Ephesians was "Did you receive the Holy Spirit when you believed?" (Acts 19:2); it proves conclusively this particular baptism in the Spirit follows salvation. At this point the preacher would do well to briefly mention the Spirit's baptism of the believer into the body of Christ at salvation and draw the distinction between it and Christ's baptism of the believer in the Spirit.

Paul reveals a certain modus operandi in his ministry to the Ephesian believers. He first made certain they had placed their hope of salvation upon Christ and then insisted upon water baptism. When he was certain the matters of salvation and water baptism had been settled, he then laid hands upon them to assist them in receiving the Baptism, which they did. This account shows the importance the Early Church placed upon the baptism in the Holy Spirit and encourages the preacher to lay hands upon believers to receive the gift of the Father. Undoubtedly, Paul learned his methods from watching the other apostles interact with believers and learned how to be effective in leading people into the baptism. Any minister of the gospel should be comfortable in using the methods and directives of the apostles.

Removing Barriers

After preachers set forth the promise of the Baptism and lay a biblical base, they need to remove misconceptions and any other barriers that keep many people from claiming the gift of the Holy Spirit. The minister should have a grasp of the questions and doubts the congregation has on the subject and should address them with clarity and authority. Some of the most prevalent are as follows:

I am not good enough to receive the baptism. This statement grows out of a flawed understanding of God's grace and Christ's righteousness. The devil loves to condemn God's children and make them feel unworthy of God's grace so they feel His promises are for everyone else but them.

It is always beneficial for a preacher to overcome false concepts with biblical truth. To overcome this barrier, the preacher should instruct his hearers on the most fundamental of all truths concerning their relationship with God, namely, faith in Christ's finished work and appropriation of His righteousness. A good question to set forth is this: "How long does it take for a person to become righteous in the sight of God?" Of course, the answer is: "As long as it takes for the believer to exchange his own righteousness, which is 'filthy rags,' for the righteousness of Christ."

Teaching on Christ's righteousness is an open door to allow the Holy Spirit to convict of sin and bring new assurances to those struggling with a sense of unworthiness. A prayer of repentance and faith is most effective to underscore the fact that no one is worthy to be saved and brought into the family of God. This is precisely why the gospel is identified as the good news of Christ.

The baptism in the Holy Spirit sounds wonderful, but it is not for me. This statement grows out of a lack of good teaching needed to differentiate between tongues as the initial physical evidence and tongues as a gift of edification.

This barrier needs to be overcome by a barrage of Scripture that proves arbitrary exclusion from God's gifts as nonbiblical and totally false. To think a loving father would play favorites by giving some of his children a wonderful gift and withholding it from others is illogical.

"God does not show favoritism."—Acts 10:34

"No good thing does he withhold from those whose walk is blameless."—Psalm 84:11

"'If you then, though you are evil, know how to give good gifts to your children, how much more will your Father in heaven give the Holy Spirit to those who ask him!'"—Luke 11:13

"The promise is for you and your children and for all who are far off—for all whom the LORD our God will call."—Acts 2:39

Critical friends of the Pentecostal experience are quick to quote Paul's asking "Do all speak in tongues?" (1 Corinthians 12:30) as proof all are not to speak in tongues. However, it is very clear that Paul is addressing public tongues and interpretation, not the gift of the Holy Spirit. Paul makes a distinction between his private prayer language of tongues and speaking in tongues in a corporate setting: "I thank God that I speak in tongues more than all of you. *But in the church* [my emphasis] I would rather speak five intelligible words to instruct others than ten thousand words in a tongue" (1 Corinthians 14:18-19).

Those who feel the baptism is not for them includes those who have sought for a long time but have never been able to take the step of faith to receive. It is helpful to remind these sincere seekers they need not wait (or "tarry") for a long time. There is no record of believers tarrying or seeking for the gift of the Holy Spirit after the initial outpouring at Pentecost (when the original waiting took place). People who are under the impression that waiting is still a part of seeking need to be instructed on how to release their faith to simply accept what God offers. The Comforter has come!

I am afraid what I receive will be of the flesh. This statement grows out of a misunderstanding about God's love and faithfulness to His children. Behind this error is a deception as old as the one perpetrated by the devil in the Garden of Eden, namely, that God cannot be trusted.

To counteract this, believers need to be reminded of their relationship to God. He is their Father, their heavenly Father, who wants to bless, not curse. Jesus' logic is conclusive: If an earthly father knows how to give good gifts, how much better the Heavenly Father is at doing so! Good fathers do not give bad things or deliberately disappoint; they do not give things like snakes and stones when a child asks for bread or fish. It is an insult to the fatherhood of God to think He would in some way double-cross one of His sincere and needy children.

It is difficult for those who grew up in Pentecost to comprehend that millions of believers in many non-Pentecostal denominations were taught from childhood that *at the very best* tongues are of the flesh. The candidate for the baptism needs to understand that there is a significant difference between something being of the flesh and something being of the Spirit using and controlling the flesh. The baptism of the Spirit comes upon the flesh and will work through the flesh to glorify God.

The only way to overcome error is by preaching truth with a total reliance upon the Spirit, and God is using His servants in the last days to strip away confusion in order to endue His people with power from on high. Many Pentecostal preachers know the validity of the promise of the Father, are strong in Pentecostal doctrine, and understand the barriers people face. Unfortunately, they are not confident in how to lead people into a process of faith that results in the infilling of the Spirit.

Among other things, one must recognize how wonderfully diverse God is in methodologies, processes, and operations. The Lord was careful in His earthly ministry not to use a single method in healing. He knew if He had used the "mud in your eye" method more than once, a cottage industry would have sprung up to make mudpacks for healing. His methods in reaching the lost varied from storytelling to proclamation to one-on-one evangelism.

A refreshing dimension of true Pentecostal worship is the potential for God's "surprises"—when He decides to change the order of service and impresses the pastor to step outside the church bulletin. The

Lord does not want the church to become dependent upon human plans and abilities. On such occasions, God may choose to pour out His Spirit in baptism unexpectedly and powerfully. Pentecostal history is replete with incidents where scores in the congregation were filled instantaneously as they were singing or an individual awoke in bed shaking under the power of God and began speaking in tongues. One minister from a non-Pentecostal denomination recently received the baptism in the Spirit and began speaking in tongues while shopping at a supermarket in Springfield, Missouri.

The unexpected is wonderful, but most of the time people receive the baptism when a minister preaches on the subject and is used by God to take candidates step-by-step into the experience. Each minister will discover a pathway of truth effective for leading people into the Baptism, but the minister must never believe a formula in and of itself will result in a person's receiving the Baptism any more than the "Roman Road" or "Evangelism Explosion" or "The Four Great Questions of Life" saves a soul. It is only when ministers recognize a method or process as a tool of the Spirit that they are free to use it.

Leading into the Baptism

In hopes of providing a tool of the Spirit, the following are suggested steps that might be taken to lead candidates into the baptism in the Spirit after the preaching of the Word:

1. The call to come forward to receive the baptism should be done in a very encouraging and non-threatening manner. Those who are hungry for the experience are often reluctant to respond publicly. Some feel like second-rate Christians because they have not received. Others may be shy. And still others fear the unknown, uncertain of what they will be asked to do.

The minister should make the appeal in such a way that, rather than feeling uncomfortable, people feel expectant about what God wants to give them. This can be accomplished by reminding seekers that most Pentecostal people were invited to respond in the very same way before they received the Holy Spirit. Tell candidates they will not be made to do anything but will simply be encouraged.

It is always helpful to have a few people ready before the service to move to the front immediately after the appeal in order to allow the believer who is reluctant to come forward feel less conspicuous. As the helpers come, it is beneficial to have the seekers form a single line to make it easier for others to join with them.

2. The call for people to join those who are coming to receive the baptism should be done with brief but important instruction. Those who are going to join faith with the seekers should themselves be filled with the Spirit and have recently spoken in tongues in prayer or praise.

It is critical that helpers be told not to try to give the Baptism to anyone. A Pentecostal cannot give any divine gift through transference or manipulation. They come around the seekers simply to create an atmosphere of praise and be an encouragement. The seeker must be taught the Lord inhabits the praises of His people. The reason Spirit-filled people are helpful to those desiring the Baptism and should stand with them is because when the church begins to praise, God comes in special habitation. Women should pray with women and men with men to avoid any kind of embarrassment or distraction.

3. When everyone is in place, the minister should ask the seekers if they are certain they are saved and in a right relationship with God. This is so important that the preacher should offer a two-part prayer: (1) Thank God for covering sin with the blood, making every believer a part of God's family. (2) Command every bit of doubt and fear be removed and in its place faith be granted to every person around the altar. Then confirm the prayer of faith by asking everyone who knows beyond a doubt they are a child of God and

qualified to receive the gift of the Spirit to raise their hands. This simple act is a way of their giving testimony and clarifying for themselves the reality and joy in being a member of the same family.

4. Explain what it means in practical terms to receive the Baptism. God the Father is offering His special gift. Point out that it is a gift. If the Baptism were earned, it would not be a gift. We receive a gift by believing it is truly being offered. Then we simply reach out and take it from the giver.

A father would be puzzled at Christmastime if one of his children was to beg for a gift he had purchased for them. Can anyone imagine a child saying, "Oh, Daddy, please give me my gift. I don't deserve it. I know it's for me, but I'm not worthy. Maybe it isn't for me . . . maybe next Christmas." An observer might think that child needed professional help. Yet many Christians keep begging their heavenly Father for a gift He has promised, has given, and even now offers.

Furthermore, everything we receive from God, we receive by faith. Faith, by its very nature, is actualizing a promise. "Faith is being sure of what we hope for and certain of what we do not see" (Hebrews 11:1). If you can see it, it does not take faith. Faith says, "I don't have possession now, but I see it; and the promise of God is the basis of my actions."

The biggest hurdle to receiving the Baptism is taking the gift by an act of the will and choosing to step out in faith, not knowing what to say but believing God will give the utterance. Many have missed the implication of the words "they . . . began to speak [they did the speaking] . . . as the Spirit gave them utterance" (Acts 2:4, KJV). It should be made obvious to candidates for the Baptism that they are going to speak, for it is quite common for seekers to stand in the presence of God with their mouths shut. To receive the Baptism, people must be encouraged to the point of faith where in essence they say, "I now receive the gift of the Holy Spirit. I am going to launch out now in a new tongue. I don't know what I am going to say; but as I begin to speak, I trust God enough to give me the utterance."

It is not necessary to lay hands upon people to receive the Baptism, but it is recorded in Acts 19 that Paul did just that in Ephesus, with the desired results. The key is to believe with people for a moment in time when they let go of their fears and begin to speak with tongues.

After a person has received the baptism, they need to be encouraged—on the spot—to believe for their prayer language. They have already spoken with tongues so, of course, their faith is high. That is the time to encourage them to exercise faith the next day to begin praying in the Spirit after they have prayed with their understanding. If they do not do that, it is highly probable they will not move into practical use and application of the Spirit-filled life. They will be content with an experience and not fulfill their potential of living with the fruit of the Spirit and ministering in the gifts of the Spirit.

Remember the Disappointed

The preacher's task is not finished after instructing those who have received the gift of the Holy Spirit. One must be very sensitive to and gentle with those who did not receive the Baptism during corporate prayer. The task is to stand firmly between the disappointed believer and the devil, who will do everything in his power to belittle and accuse of unbelief. The preacher can turn a negative situation into positive faith.

Those who have not received the Baptism need to be told they will receive if they keep reaching out to claim the promise. God is not about to cancel His promises. All God's children have their faith tested, but the promises of God remain.

It is often helpful to those who are struggling to receive the gift of the Spirit to hear a testimony from someone who went through the same struggle. Every Pentecostal pastor knows of incidents where people left the altar and received the Baptism on the way home or the next day during private devotions. It is critical that people maintain their hunger for the infilling of the Spirit; assure them they cannot be denied any gift or blessing God has promised to His children.

Preaching on the subject of the baptism in the Holy Spirit and leading people into the experience is one of the greatest privileges afforded Pentecostal preachers. They know the unsurpassed joy of introducing believers to a fullness in Christ that will change their lives forever.

Chapter 11

Preaching on Spiritual Gifts

The apostle Paul's desire that the church be schooled in the gifts of the Holy Spirit must be a concern of every Pentecostal preacher. If Pentecostals do not preach and teach on the subject, who will? By default it will fall to non-Pentecostals, those who do not have a personal experience of being baptized in the Spirit with the initial physical evidence of speaking with tongues. In addition, most non-Pentecostals do not believe in the operation of spiritual gifts. Just as we would not accept a non-Christian as an authority on the subject of personal salvation, it follows that those who have not had a Pentecostal experience do not have the same authority as those who have.

Spiritual gifts are extremely important for many reasons. They are a provision by the Lord himself to equip the Church in the area of supernatural works. They are biblical in faith and practice. They are a means to edify the body of Christ corporately and minister miracles to and through believers individually. They are a powerful witness to the unsaved. They are a mighty spiritual standard against the subtlety of the devil and the onslaughts of hell. The Church needs the full operation of spiritual gifts as much today as any time in history.

Sound, biblical, Spirit-filled teaching on the value and operation of the gifts of the Spirit is a classic example of overcoming evil with good. Admittedly the topic has been fraught with so much misinformation, misunderstanding, and misapplication many preachers have thrown up their hands and chosen to avoid it. But if the gifts were not vital to the life of the church, they would not be part of biblical doctrine and practice. The proper use of spiritual gifts is a blessed provision and glorious blessing that far outweighs any possible negative consequences. Contemporary Pentecostal preachers must understand potential dangers and abuses—and then set out to correct them.

Four Great Obstacles

There are four great obstacles the preacher must overcome in the area of spiritual gifts. Paul was very conscious of them, but none of them dissuaded him from recognizing the value of these gifts and insisting upon their being operational in the local congregation.

1. The first obstacle is ignorance. "Now about spiritual gifts, brothers, I do not want you to be ignorant" (1 Corinthians 12:1). Paul was addressing believers and, in this case, Pentecostals. The ignorance he feared was not so much a lack of knowledge but a lack of understanding, or wisdom.

Other translations of 1 Corinthians 12:1 shed light on the kind of ignorance Paul is concerned with: "I want to clear up a wrong impression about spiritual gifts" (JB). "I want you to know the truth about them" (TEV). "I don't want any misunderstanding about them" (TLB). "I want to give you some further information in spiritual matters" (Phillips). "I do not want you to be uninformed" (RSV).

Sadly, Paul would find a great deal of the same ignorance and misunderstanding about spiritual gifts in the churches today he found in the church at Corinth. It would not be difficult to find Pentecostal churches in America that know almost nothing about the gifts of the Spirit or have wrong views about them.

2. The second obstacle is fear. "No one who is speaking by the Spirit of God says, 'Jesus be cursed'"

(1 Corinthians 12:3). Paul knew his congregation well. They had come out of a demonic culture and had been misled by idolatry, false religion, and carnal impulses. They had a residual fear of being swept away again into error. They were terrified of being duped and deceived.

The Pentecostal preacher of today has to address the same fear Paul addressed in the Corinthian church. People coming into a Pentecostal fellowship hear believers claiming to speak messages by the Spirit of God. How can they know whether what they are hearing is of God or not? Paul is quick to identify one sure test: The Spirit of God, which is the Spirit of truth and revelation, always glorifies the Lord Jesus Christ; God's Spirit would never curse or denigrate the Son.

The safety net for all believers in both faith and practice is the centrality of Jesus Christ. Any faith which lessens the place of Christ is a false faith. Any spiritual activity that takes away from His lordship is at best carnal and at worst demonic. Wherever the Pentecostal church has endured, it has done so because its theology and teaching have been Christ-centered, both in spirit and in word.

Fear of Pentecost has been perpetuated by those who insist upon pointing to excesses and abuses in Pentecost but at the same time do not insist upon finding and maintaining true Pentecost. Sincere people who fear the baptism in the Spirit is not of God will have fear replaced by faith once they witness a true Baptism and its resulting love and fervor for Christ.

3. The third obstacle is apathy. "Eagerly desire the greater gifts" (1 Corinthians 12:31; compare 2 Timothy 1:6). Paul knew the church could become indifferent to spiritual gifts; hence, his admonition to believers to set their hearts upon receiving and exercising "the greater gifts."

There is a clear and present danger in Pentecost of losing focus and intentionality concerning spiritual gifts. One reason is the proliferation of so many good things, which can crowd out the highest and best. The church calendar is full of wonderful programs, wholesome activities, special events, and social action. Therefore, the critical question to ask about the church calendar is not how many activities it contains but the spiritual priorities those activities reflect. Furthermore, the preacher must protect the pulpit and be proactive in declaring the whole counsel of God—which will include a regular emphasis on the gifts of the Spirit. If the apostle Paul were to visit Pentecostal churches today, would he be pleased to see congregations heeding the command to "eagerly desire the greater gifts," or would he be disappointed and alarmed?

4. The fourth obstacle is pride. This is by far the greatest threat to the proper use of the gifts of the Spirit. On the one hand, pride produces the kind of embarrassing behavior that causes most of the criticisms of Pentecostals by non-Pentecostals. On the other hand, pride, a fear of who may be visiting the church, keeps Pentecostals from wanting to demonstrate gifts of the Spirit. They are not aware of the large number of people who were brought to God, became Pentecostal, and joined the church because they witnessed the power of God through the proper demonstration of spiritual gifts.

Paul was very much aware of the destructive force of pride and was careful to teach on the subject of spiritual gifts within a context of humility and love, the antitheses of pride.

It is instructive to note that the subjects of the Cross and Communion precede Paul's teaching on spiritual gifts. After dealing with the matter of Communion in 1 Corinthians 11, Paul opens Chapter 12 with these words: "Now about spiritual gifts." It is as if he were saying, "Now that I have dealt with the necessity of believers' examining their hearts in the light of Christ's broken body and shed blood, they are ready to receive direction in spiritual gifts. Without a proper attitude, which can come only from a crucified self, these believers will become spiritually proud and cancel all the effectiveness of spiritual gifts."

When Paul does introduce the subject of spiritual gifts in Chapter 12, he reminds the Corinthians how vulnerable they are to deception and how dependent they must be upon the Holy Spirit. He then proceeds to state the facts concerning spiritual gifts (vv. 4-10). With verse 11, he begins a lengthy dissertation on unity, which takes the rest of Chapter 12. Paul is wisely teaching that spiritual gifts should result in unity, whereas pride could fracture a congregation (which is one of the most frequent criticisms by non-Pentecostals).

Love, the Hallmark

Before Paul begins his detailed instructions on tongues in 1 Corinthians 14, he introduces the importance of love, the hallmark of a true Pentecostal church. All spiritual gifts, ministries, operations, sacrifices, and talents are effective only if they are exercised or applied in a spirit of love.

Without love, all the gifts of the Spirit become ends in themselves rather than tools and enablements for building the church. Paul knew some of the less-than-humble believers would grasp for spiritual prestige through offices, titles, and gifts of the Spirit. He makes clear all of these things are necessary because God makes the appointments. However, no one needs a title to exercise gifts, but everyone must operate in love in order for the church to be strong.

The "most excellent way" introduced in 1 Corinthians 12:31 is not a repudiation of the gifts. To the contrary, it is a way to enhance the gifts. Without operating in love, all human effort is canceled and the gifts of God are diminished. Spiritual gifts can divide but love always unites. Anyone who has been in Pentecost for any length of time has witnessed those who operate the gifts without love and those who operate them with love. There would be universal agreement those who love have discovered the "most excellent way" to build God's kingdom. An excellent spirit is necessary to do God's work effectively.

Nearly everything worthwhile in the church has its

risks because of human instrumentality. For instance, some pastors have failed to add full-time personnel, ministry gifts, because they are insecure and feel a staff or an associate is not worth the trouble. They have witnessed another pastor who has gone through grief because of an errant staff member. So instead of doing what is best for the church, they have become prisoners of the fear of what might happen. In spite of the potential dangers and possible abuses, all the Spirit's gifts not only are worth the risk but are to be coveted and encouraged.

Gifts of the Spirit and their operation are biblical and needed in the Pentecostal church. They basically define a Pentecostal church. The debate going on today about the difference between what constitutes a classic Pentecostal church or a charismatic church or a contemporary Pentecostal church will never be settled, because the debate is over nonbiblical nomenclature. The wrong question is being asked. The question should be: "What is a biblical Pentecostal church?" The answer is quite simple. It is a Great Commission church that operates in the power of the Holy Spirit, encouraging all the supernatural gifts and ministries God has provided.

As preachers approach the subject of spiritual gifts, they should come with a sense of excitement and faith, not foreboding and unbelief. They need to come in the fear of God, not man. They should look upon the gifts of the Spirit as nonnegotiable in a Pentecostal context. All Pentecostal preachers have a responsibility to make the gifts of the Spirit an important part of the belief system and lifestyle of the church because they are a part of God's provision. The fear of people has taken away too many blessings from the church. Let it never be said that negative statements or criticism by the uninformed or misled determined the Pentecostal message.

What are the gifts of the Spirit? They are manifestations of the Spirit in the form of supernatural embodiments and abilities. They are not to be confused with natural talent, no matter how brilliant or impressive.

First Corinthians 12:8-10 lists nine gifts of the Spirit. Is this an exhaustive list or representative? It is always dangerous to box God into a set number of anything, especially in this case when verse 4 says "there are different kinds of gifts." Preachers would be on solid ground to teach that the Spirit has revealed some of the vital and more common gifts of the Spirit; but because there is no stated limitation as to the number, no one should say God could not bestow others. As Dr. Stanley Horton rhetorically asks in *What the Bible Says about the Holy Spirit*, "How can there be any limit to the abundance of His gifts that are available for the fellowship, life, and work of the Church?" However, because these nine are listed, preachers are responsible to inform and teach their congregations about them.

The Word of Wisdom

The first gift is the *word of wisdom*. The original Greek for "word" is *logos*, the same as found in John 1:1. Surprisingly, most modern translations take great liberties, to the point of changing or stretching its meaning. For instance, the New International Version originally (1973) interpreted "the word of wisdom" as "the ability to speak with wisdom" (now "the message of wisdom"). The Living Bible says "the ability to give wise advice." The Jerusalem Bible says "the gift of preaching with wisdom." The Revised Standard Version comes closest to logos: "the utterance of wisdom." The King James and New King James versions translate the pure value of logos and simply state "the word of wisdom."

In understanding the gift of the word of wisdom, the King James Version serves the preacher well because it removes complications and ambiguities raised by other translations. Simply stated, the gift of the word of wisdom is a supernatural enablement to make the best use of knowledge. It is a powerful gift to the church, especially when leadership has knowledge of facts but does not know how to use them in a given situation.

Many times throughout Pentecostal history, both on a local and national level, God has given deliberative bodies clear direction through unlikely people. The Early Church was a direct beneficiary of this wonderful gift. When the disciples were confronting unprecedented church growth and found themselves neglecting prayer and study of the Word, they were given a divine solution: Appoint seven Spirit-filled men to see to the duties of caring for widows. The result was a multiplication of the church (Acts 6:1-7). As we shall see, there are moments of great faith when God demands bold steps beyond what is seen; but often the spirit is a spirit of prudence and deliberate thought.

The Book of Acts is a testimony to the faithfulness of the Holy Spirit in giving wise counsel, from sending faith workers and missionaries (13:2; 15:22) to giving insight in how to respond to Gentile believers (15:19-21; 16:1-3).

The Holy Spirit continues to give supernatural wisdom to Pentecostal denominations and local churches who are dependent upon divine direction. Several years ago, the board of the church I was pastoring was prepared to recommend the purchase of a city block and a larger building for a new church site. Before the meeting, a very wonderful brother came to me and said, "Pastor, in prayer this morning the Lord impressed upon me to tell you it would be wisdom to make a further study of the proposed property." Something in my spirit witnessed this man had heard from God. I put a hold on the project and asked for a small committee to review every detail of the proposal. While they were working on the assignment, a far better piece of property surfaced at a "miracle" price. Later we discovered the original property had some serious environmental problems that would have cost our congregation hundreds of thousands of dollars.

The Bible speaks of increasing knowledge as a sign

of the last days. Unfortunately, there is not a promise of increasing wisdom. However, the Pentecostal church can seek and expect to receive special wisdom in critical moments of decision.

The gift of the word of wisdom guards against our "good [being] spoken of as evil" (Romans 14:16). In a day when there are myriads of choices, the Pentecostal church needs God's wisdom as never before. The cause of Christ has suffered unnecessarily at the hands of many sincere and well-meaning people who believed because something looked good, it was good for them; or because something looked right, it was right for them—right now. The consequences have been disastrous. Had the Builder of the Church been consulted, He would have given a word of wisdom contrary to human wisdom.

Many Pentecostal pastors have been needlessly embarrassed by well-meaning and sincere believers who have taken it upon themselves to attack publications on major issues without studying facts and preparing presentations with wisdom and a Christlike spirit. The Pentecostal church must speak to vital issues in such a way as not to bring an unnecessary reproach on the gospel. The disciples were labeled "unschooled, ordinary men" but they were so filled with the Holy Spirit and wisdom their enemies knew "these men had been with Jesus."

The Word of Knowledge

The second gift of the Spirit is the word of knowledge. The gift of the word of knowledge is a body of information or an awareness of facts that can be known only by a supernatural revelation. It is not to be confused with "a knowledgeable person" or someone with great formal education.

A word of knowledge is needed when truth is needed but not known. It is in the context in which Paul says to the church over and over: "Did you not know?" He was battling what all Pentecostal leaders battle: the conflict between the carnal mind and the mind of

Christ. A word of divine knowledge can come only through a mind open to revelation knowledge and not limited by sensual or human knowledge.

When preaching on the gift of the word of knowledge, the preacher needs to be familiar with the extreme teachings on all the gifts. For example, some have transferred the role of the gift to the individual, when clearly it is primarily for the building up of the body. The danger is evident when people claim to have a *rhema* word from God for someone but do not have others to judge whether the word is of divine or human origins. Many sincere believers have been destroyed by "super spiritual" people who have become so proud they bristle at any correction or rebuke. However, proper guidance in the use of gifts is precisely the responsibility of spiritual elders. How much better for a leader to be accused of "quenching the Spirit" than for a believer to be confused by an unrestrained, bearer of spurious knowledge.

The need for a true revival of the gift of the word of knowledge can hardly be overstated. The spiritual leader above all should realize how dependent the body of Christ is upon the direction of the Holy Spirit. It is the truth needed, the path revealed, and the bridge from the known to the unknown. It is the Spirit's cry: "This is the way; walk in it" (Isaiah 30:21).

The Gift of Faith

The third gift is faith. It is a supernatural confidence in God for a particular situation. It is a very special gift to the church for the purpose of confronting the impossible with divine boldness.

The preacher has the task of clearly differentiating between "ordinary" faith and "extraordinary faith." The Bible says, "Without faith it is impossible to please God" (Hebrews 11:6). Jesus rebuked His disciples for lack of faith. Evidently there is a consistent faith for which believers are responsible. This is the faith that grows by taking in the Word and applying truth day by day. Pentecostal people must be taught their responsibility to grow their faith. They are not to seek a gift of faith as a substitute for a mature faith growing out of spiritual disciplines.

On occasion, a congregation's normal faith may confront a difficulty so great they are tempted to settle for the difficulty and adjust to its consequences. At the same time, God can breathe extraordinary faith into a believer or an entire congregation, and the gift of faith moves the hand of God in extraordinary power. For example, there is "mountain climbing" faith that requires ordinary faith, and then there is "mountain moving" faith that requires a special enduement of faith by the Spirit.

The gift of faith is available to the church and needs to be proclaimed as a divine resource. Surely this is one of the "best gifts" (KJV) the church should covet and receive. There is a perception that churches in third world countries routinely enjoy mighty miracles because they have "simple" faith. Could it be that they simply believe God's Word and have a mindset that allows God's Spirit to gift them with special faith? God has not canceled His promise nor experienced a reduction of His power. This should encourage every Pentecostal to believe for a gift of faith and every preacher to foster the atmosphere that welcomes it.

If the Pentecostal church would begin to truly covet the gift of faith for the challenges of our present day culture, we would begin having more and more testimonies of healing and deliverance.

Gifts of Healing

The fourth gift is the gifts of healing. This manifestation is a supernatural touch of God that reverses sickness and disease. It is not the state of good health, which is a wonderful blessing. It is also different from the gift of miracles. Of course, one can experience a miracle of divine healing. In that case, the miracle bypasses the process of healing and restores the person in an extraordinarily short time.

The Pentecostal church has always been known for its emphasis upon divine healing. In spite of that fact, the contemporary Pentecostal preacher needs to address this subject often to build faith and correct misconceptions. One temptation in this day of "instant gratification" is to deny God's healing power if there are no immediate results. Many who have been healed have testified that they "felt nothing" or "became worse" at the time; however, they were given special faith and despite negative symptoms knew they were healed. That kind of faith needs to be encouraged and not denigrated, because the very nature of faith is being "certain of what we do not see."

The preacher must not look upon doctors and medicines as reasons for unbelief but rather as resources for healing—divine healing; God often uses such resources. A pastor's wife experienced pain for years. No tests surfaced the source. The pastor joined her in faith and prayed for a miracle of healing or a *path* to healing. After prayer, the problem was discovered, and God used a skilled surgeon to begin the process of complete restoration.

It should be noted that in the wisdom of God, He did not give a gift of healing to a person but gives gifts—plural—of healing as He chooses. There are individuals who are more open to faith for healing than others but they are not given a resident gift of healing. Nor is it proper—no matter how effective a ministry might be in healing—to call anyone a divine healer. At best, an individual is a channel for God's healing power.

Pentecostal preachers must maintain a spirit of humility and honesty when addressing the subject of divine healing. They need to point out God is not limited to a method or timeline. Jesus certainly brought gifts of healing, but He chose many methods. He simply spoke the word of healing in the case of the centurion servant (Matthew 8:13). He simply touched the hand of Peter's mother-in-law (Matthew 8:15). The woman with the issue of blood touched the hem of

Jesus' garment (Mark 5:27-28). Jesus made clay from spittle to heal a blind man (John 9:6). In one case He touched a man twice to complete the healing (Mark 8:24,25).

The disciples learned these lessons of divine healing well, for they did not rely upon any one method either. Peter took the lame man at the Beautiful Gate by the hand (Acts 3:7), but his shadow was enough for others (Acts 5:15). And Paul used handkerchiefs and aprons as a point of contact for healing (Acts 19:12).

Working of Miracles

The fifth gift of the Spirit is the working of miracles. Pentecostal preachers should be in their element when preaching and practicing this gift because it is a natural outgrowth of the explosive power (Greek *dunamis*, giving us the word "dynamite") Christ promised His Church after His ascension.

The opening of the twenty-first century presents the greatest opportunity in church history for the American church to release the power of God by believing the awesome declarations of Jesus: "Anyone who has faith in me will do what I have been doing. He will do even greater things" (John 14:12) and "These signs will accompany those who believe" (Mark 16:17). His promise was fulfilled by the Early Church. The Book of Acts is filled with disciples given great power to perform miracles. Today, our world stands ready to see a miracle-working church again. Weary of theory, groping and hoping, this generation is ready for a ministry that is not limited by darkened thought and cynical unbelief.

One of the greatest tools for church growth in the American Pentecostal church is a return to the miraculous. No human resource can build the true kingdom. It is going to take an army of ministers who will confront this culture not with words of human wisdom but, like Paul, "with a demonstration of the Spirit's power" (1 Corinthians 2:4).

The only thing that stopped Jesus, the ultimate miracle worker, from performing the works of God in greater number was unbelief. Where did that unbelief develop? In the place where Christ was known—in His home country and in the place where truth should have been proclaimed in such a way as to build great faith, namely, in the synagogue. It is sobering to note Jesus did great miracles where He was not well known and demon power was in control. May it be said of the twenty-first century Pentecostal church that its faith did not rest in human wisdom but in the power of God because it ministered a supernatural word followed by miraculous works.

The matter needs to be put before every Pentecostal preacher. The gift of miraculous works are available to the Church of Jesus Christ. You are a catalyst of faith and a preacher of truth. If you are not performing miraculous works, when are you going to start? When the pulpit answers in faith, "Now!" America will witness a mighty move of God.

Gift of Prophecy

The sixth gift is prophecy—perhaps the most misunderstood of all the gifts because of some confusion about its roles and purpose in the contemporary Pentecostal church.

The definition of the word "prophecy" has a plural meaning. In its simplest terms, it means to foretell or forth-tell. It means to predict the future by divine inspiration, and it also means to speak for God by declaring His Word.

In the Old Testament, the office of the prophet can be likened to the role of the ordained Pentecostal preacher. There were some who were known for their ability to predict the future, but it seems the vast majority were trained in proclaiming the Word of God. Undoubtedly, the School of the Prophets was nothing more than an ancient Bible institute.

The prophets of old had a role in writing the Scriptures and in laying foundational truth for the

Church, but the prophetic ministry in the New Testament and beyond was prosecuted primarily through those God ordained to proclaim His Word in authority. First Corinthians 14:1 tells us to desire the greater gifts; to speak the Word of God with anointing (that is, prophecy) is the greater and more consistent way the Lord of the church edifies His people and builds His church.

On the Day of Pentecost, the gift of tongues was clearly evident and resulted in great interest, but no one was converted until Peter stood and preached with prophetic power. The gift of tongues was a supernatural sign, but the prophetic word was the means of saving truth.

The gift of prophecy, when put in context, is quite simple to grasp. It is a supernatural utterance in a native tongue that edifies the church corporately. On occasion laypeople speak prophetically. However, most often it is God-anointed preachers who go beyond their own thought processes to the point where it is clear to everyone that what they are hearing is not "so says man" but "so says the Lord." It is the flow of the Spirit as He gives the proclaimer utterance.

The gift of prophecy in the New Testament context is basically anointed preaching and speaking. This fact is borne out in 1 Corinthians 14:3 when the function of supernatural forth-telling leads to strengthening, encouragement, and comfort.

The preacher must recognize the value of prophecy as a dimension of his ministry. The impact of false interpretations of Scripture fed by moral relativism demands that the nation hear the true Word of the Lord. Darkened minds are taking the Word of God and twisting it to say what they want it to say. The power of a man or woman speaking under the anointing of the Holy Spirit is the light that will overcome darkness.

The fact the gift of prophecy is a corporate gift for the edification of the church rules out personal prophecy as a biblical methodology. Furthermore, the gift of prophecy, as all other gifts, is subject to judgment by spiritual elders who judge whether the word spoken is contrary to the Scripture or the Spirit of Jesus. There are enough safeguards to protect God's people, and when they are observed, the Holy Spirit maximizes the effectiveness of the prophetic word.

The Discerning of Spirits

The seventh gift of the Spirit is discerning of spirits. The supernatural discernment of spirits is one of God's enablements to protect the church from the enemy and his deception. Like all the gifts, it is not human ability nor is it through a process of education or training; it is given instantly when needed.

Without the gift of discerning of spirits in the Pentecostal church today, there will be a growing number of confused and disillusioned believers because of the multiplicity of messages influencing the mind. Modern technology has brought its blessings, but it has also brought dangers our forefathers never faced. The avenues for deception are many.

Preachers of today must arm those under their guidance to know and be aware of Satan's devices and, at the same time, give biblical teaching concerning supernatural discernment. The Church of God need never be a victim of satanic spirits because the Spirit has come to empower it with *drakrisis* (Greek), meaning literally "judging through." It is the ability to "see right through" someone who is motivated by or operating with the wrong spirit.

Jesus Christ used the discerning of spirits on many occasions during His earthly ministry, which should be the role model for every Pentecostal preacher. When He called His disciple Nathanael, He discerned he was "a true Israelite, in whom there is nothing false" (John 1:47). He also reprimanded His disciples for the wrong spirit: "You do not know what manner of spirit you are of" (Luke 9:54-55, NKJV). Certainly Peter felt the stern rebuke of our Lord when He said to him, "Get behind me, Satan" (Matthew 16:23).

Christ's ability to cast out demons was preceded by His ability to know the spirits.

The Early Church was given the gift of discerning of spirits. The young church was sobered by the ability of Peter to "see through" the facade of Ananias and Sapphira (Acts 5), and the inhabitants of Paphos by the ability of Paul to confront Elymas the sorcerer (Acts 13). The disciples were also given power over demons and were able to confront them with authority because they were given special discernment.

The serious student will be quick to observe the discerning of spirits in the ministries of Christ and the disciples was primarily to build up and edify the church. In the past, many Pentecostals have limited this marvelous gift just to demonic spirits, but God wants to restore the full power of this gift to the church in order to reprove and rebuke those within the church who have a wrong spirit toward others, which, unless revealed and checked, will result in division.

Different Kinds of Tongues

The eighth gift is different kinds of tongues, the ability to speak supernaturally in languages unknown to the speaker. This marvelous gift has many purposes. By itself (without interpretation), it edifies the believer through divine communication with God. It is used by God as a sign to the unbeliever who hears someone speak his or her language only to discover that the speaker has never learned the language.

Tongues as a sign to the unbeliever were evident on the Day of Pentecost and have continued throughout church history, especially in the area of world missions in the last hundred years. Many have come to Christ through the exercise of this gift.

There are those who believe tongues were limited to the apostolic age and are only for a sign to the unbeliever. These limitations fly in the face of the New Testament record and biblical teaching on the gift of tongues. Tongues were spoken in the presence of believers. In 1 Corinthians 12 and 14, Paul is careful to admonish believers on how to exercise the gift in the church.

The twenty-first century Pentecostal church faces a great challenge. A growing number of charismatic/ Pentecostal scholars are attacking tongues as the initial physical evidence on the basis that it does not come up to their standard of biblical doctrine. Preachers, however, are not beholden to what people may conclude; they are ordained by God to preach the Word through the revelation of the Spirit and to make known the wonderful works of God. Tongues are not only a sign to those who don't believe; they are also a gift for every one who does believe. May Bible preachers never be guilty of shortchanging their congregations by setting aside this divine enablement.

Interpretation of Tongues

The ninth gift of the Spirit is the interpretation of tongues. While tongues by themselves are a gift to the individual believer and a sign to the unbeliever, the interpretation of tongues is reserved for the edification of the church.

In a practical sense, tongues with interpretation is equal to prophecy because it is supernatural "forth telling" from God through human channels. Being a form of prophecy, tongues with interpretation is one of the best gifts the church should covet and practice.

Pentecostal preachers have been given the responsibility to guide the church in the use of all the gifts, especially the vocal gifts, because wonderful, sincere people can innocently cause confusion if they are not trained in when and how to exercise them. Pentecostal people need to be taught that rules do not rule out a gift of the Spirit. Only the flesh and an unscriptural message are ruled out, and truly spiritual people would want to be corrected.

According to 1 Corinthians 12 and 14, tongues and interpretation are to be part of a Pentecostal church service. When one speaks in tongues in the congregation, he is to pray that he may interpret (1 Corinthians

14:13). The norm should be for the speaker to interpret, but there are times when one speaks and another interprets. The leader of the meeting has the task along with spiritual elders to judge the interpretation and confirm its validity. First Corinthians 14:27 and 29 place a limit on the number of tongues and interpretations or prophetic utterances in a meeting. Such scriptural counsel is meant to protect the congregation from a misuse of this gift. Thus when a minister applies biblical guidelines for the use of this gift, the church is blessed and edified.

Pentecostals have been judged harshly for the obvious misuse and extremes of gifts. That judgment is justified because God has subjected His ministry gifts in the church to scriptural practice and divine order. When the preacher will not fulfill this God-given trust of leadership, the gifts slip into chaos, manifestations of the Spirit become manifestations of the flesh, and the unbeliever is adversely influenced, possibly to the point of rejecting Christ and His Church.

Pentecostal preaching is incomplete when it does not proclaim and promote the gifts of the Spirit. The enemy desires the pulpit downplay, mute, and ultimately ignore the supernatural. Church history is a record in part of revival movements that earnestly sought and embraced the miraculous and then slowly began to doubt them, so that today they even deny the Word of God. Consequently, the gifts of the Spirit are not only available to the church, they are also desperately needed—all of them. The future of the Pentecostal movement may very well be determined by how Pentecostal preachers proclaim these gifts and encourage their congregations to manifest them.

Chapter 12

Preparing a Pentecostal Message

Many good books have been written on the subject of sermon preparation and preaching. And certainly ministers can gain great insight and sharpen their effectiveness through studying others. But no one can learn to be a great Pentecostal preacher through books or tapes alone, because preaching is so personal and unique.

A Pentecostal message has a supernatural dimension beyond the ability of a human being to define, let alone reproduce. At the same time, there is a part that preachers can be responsible for, and that responsibility demands mental and spiritual excellence every time they proclaim the Word of the Lord. Only when preachers realize they must do their part in prayer and study will God be pleased to do His part through them. The old tongue-in-cheek expression "The harder I work, the luckier I get" could be changed when referring to Pentecostal preaching to "The harder I work, the more God works."

First, The Messenger

Preparation for a Pentecostal message begins with the preparation of a Pentecostal messenger. In a very real sense, the preacher is the message. If people do not have confidence in and respect for the person in the pulpit, if that person is not reliable, then the

189

message becomes distorted. If the preacher's divine authority can be undermined or his integrity called into question, then his message can be undermined. The antidote to this very real possibility is a constant reliance upon the power of the Holy Spirit. The command to be "filled with the Spirit" (Ephesians 5:18) has a special meaning and urgency for the minister of God.

A friend of mine who has preached almost 50 years recalls his night of ordination. An old pastor with a sterling reputation and a long record of success as a powerful preacher placed his hands on the head of my friend, looked up to heaven, and prayed, "Oh, God, keep him full of the Holy Ghost!" That old preacher had learned the secret of success for any preacher.

The beginning of sermon preparation for a Pentecostal minister does not begin with a pen, a computer, or even a Bible. It begins at the Throne of Grace and in an Upper Room. One of the unavoidable facts preachers face is their humanity and carnality. Such inherent weaknesses are overcome by repentance and confession, followed by the Holy Spirit's renewal of heart and mind.

Find the Mind of Christ

It is foolhardy and nonproductive for Pentecostal preachers to prepare for the pulpit with a proud heart and a carnal mind. Still, the temptation comes to "get something for Sunday," dig around in some old notes, or listen to a tape or read a book until "something" strikes them as preachable. The same thing can happen in reading the Bible as a sermon source. What is missing is the mind of Christ. When the human mind is not under the control of the Spirit, truth is interpreted in a carnal frame-work, resulting in a sermon from human understanding rather than divine revelation and insight.

Pentecostal preachers need to take God's warnings very seriously. They steer the minister of the Word away from the wrong thought processes. "The letter kills," Scripture declares (2 Corinthians 3:6). Add the fact "to be carnally minded is death" (Romans 8:6,

KJV) and the result is a prescription for spiritual disaster. The carnally minded preacher is a purveyor of death rather than life.

The written Word of God is inspired and infallible. Even so, to those not born of the Spirit of God, it is a foreign language. They attempt to compare the spiritual with the carnal and try to interpret divine truth through a secular paradigm. The words have no meaning to them because they are separated from the viewpoint of the Author.

Too much weight is placed upon words as ends in themselves without dependence upon the Holy Spirit. As a Pentecostal preacher, I have to constantly guard against thinking sermon preparation is done when my manuscript is finished, as if the right arrangement of words can speak conviction and life. The statement "No one who is speaking by the Spirit of God says, 'Jesus be cursed,' and no one can say, 'Jesus is Lord,' except by the Holy Spirit" (1 Corinthians 12:3) has been mentioned in this book. It is a vital statement. The words "Jesus is Lord" is inspired and infallible; but it cannot be said in truth apart from the revelation of the Spirit.

The Word of God is not safe in the hands of preachers with a personal agenda; they will inevitably use the Scriptures to support self-interest, not the kingdom of God. The only remedy for the spirit of death and deception coming from the pulpit is the Spirit of Truth, because it is not in rebellion against God who declared it. The carnal mind is an enemy of divine truth. It is like rebellious children who want their parents' word to mean something other than what was clearly stated.

When preachers are filled with the Spirit, their minds are in tune with the will of God. Their desire is not only to be true to what God literally said in His Word but also to interpret the meaning or intention behind that Word. It translates the "timely" from the timeless. Having the mind of Christ means never contradicting the text; it means using the text to say not only "This is what the Lord says" but also "This is what the Lord means at this moment or in this circumstance."

Ready to Begin the Process

When the heart is right and the anointing of the Spirit is upon the mind, the preacher is ready to approach the process that will lead to an effective message. This is done in total submission to God in an attitude of prayer. The Pentecostal has a wonderful resource in praying in the Spirit because the Spirit helps human weakness; this includes not knowing how to pray, for then the Holy Spirit consents to take over and pray through the yielded vessel.

The Spirit-filled preacher will be guided supernaturally to the message God wants proclaimed. There is nothing mysterious or complex about this process. If the preacher is truly filled with the Spirit, then the mind, will, brain, and common sense are under divine authority and control. What appears to be natural will really be supernatural. An impression to preach exegetically through a book of the Bible is really not an impression but divine direction. A desire to address a topic on a given Sunday will not be the preacher's desire alone but the will of the Holy Spirit. This is the normal pattern, and the Spirit honors that process. It is rare for the Spirit of God to direct a minister to leave a determined direction or a prepared message. Pentecostal preachers need to be reminded the Holy Spirit anoints plans, mental disciplines, and hard work. Saying that does not preclude the Holy Spirit from setting aside normal processes and using the unexpected to do a mighty work.

I have been a Pentecostal preacher for over forty years. Only four times in all those years has the Spirit of God impressed me to lay aside a prepared message and preach extemporaneously. Yes, God did a special work in those present on each of those occasions, but the greatest work was done in my heart. I was reminded God has the final word in everything—even when I had written down the "final word" of my sermon.

Blessed is the preacher who approaches sermon preparation with faith and enthusiasm rather than fear and dread. To know the message itself will be anointed is indeed a blessing, but to know the hours of preparation can be hours of communion with God filled with flashes of insight and divine revelation is glory!

The preacher should always open the Word of God with a sense of faith. The hours spent in preparing a message is not a waste; it is the pursuit of truth that will be used of God to change the eternal destinies of the lost and make a profound difference in the lives of believers.

Because preaching is communication through human personality, it is logical to assume every preacher has a uniqueness about his preaching, including the length of time and methodologies used in preparation. Because of that fact, this chapter is more suggestive than directive. However, much of what is suggested must be done in one way or another to reach the goal of creating a manuscript from which to preach.

One of the weaknesses in much Pentecostal preaching in the past has come from a reluctance to write out sermons. This fear of being in the flesh often resulted in preaching a message not worth writing down. How a preacher uses the manuscript is immaterial (I have never preached with notes, let alone a manuscript), but the manuscript is silent proof the preacher has labored in the Word and has sought to rightly divide the Word of truth to the best of his ability under the guidance of the Holy Spirit. After all, men wrote as they were moved upon by the Spirit. That is the reason we have the Scriptures and that is the reason we have a record of memorable sermons.

The process begins after spiritual preparation of the heart and a topic or portion of Scripture is in focus for study and development. For the purpose of clarity and the best use of time, I recommend the following steps:

Amassing the Material

It has often been said teachers always learn more in preparation than what the student learns in the presentation. The same can be said of the preacher. It is in the research and gathering of material that a wonderful, serendipitous result takes place.

Since Pentecostal preachers are Bible preachers, whatever is preached must be within the context of Scripture. If the sermon is topical, what the Bible says about the topic is the foundation. If the sermon is exegetical, the message will stay within the perimeters of the text. This reminder should not need to be made—all too often, however, the Bible is not the centerpiece of preparation. Some preachers are more concerned about making someone else's outline work rather than being concerned about correctly handling the Word of truth.

During a lecture of the late English expositor Dr. Martyn Lloyd-Jones, I was amused to hear him comment on the lack of originality in modern-day preaching. He was convinced published sermons and tapes had ruined many preachers. (I enjoyed his lecture so much I bought the tape!) His concern had some validity. If one makes a habit of using other preachers' sermons, one will eventually become spiritually lazy in preparation and shallow in preaching.

Study the Scripture First

Study the Scripture first. With an open Bible, begin the process of understanding the context of your text. The old adage "A text without a context is a pretext" is still valid. In topical preaching, carefully research and cross-reference what the Scripture says on the subject. In exegetical preaching, read the chapters on either side of the passage you plan to develop.

Sermons of spiritual depth are a result of in-depth study. Donald Grey Barnhouse was known as a great Bible preacher. Many years ago he was a guest lecturer in my homiletics class. He told us he would use every opportunity to travel to and from Europe on a ship because it gave him uninterrupted time to study the Word of God. With great enthusiasm, he shared the experience of his last voyage: reading the Book of

Philippians slowly more than one hundred times while making notations.

Let the Holy Spirit speak into your own spirit as you read the context. The directive to each of the churches in Revelation is good counsel to the preacher: "He who has an ear, let him hear what the Spirit says to the churches" (2:7). The preacher must cultivate a spiritual ear to receive the truth. The fact is the Spirit is talking. He is speaking. He is commenting on the written Word. Of all people, the Pentecostal preacher should be receptive to the One who "will guide . . . into all truth" (John 16:13).

As the Spirit Speaks

As the Spirit speaks through insight, impression, conviction, and revelation, write down the thoughts that come to you without concern for structure or priority. When the context is clear, move to the text itself. Read the text from different translations. Study the meaning of key words. Read the text from the perspective of the young and the old. Look at it through the prism of history and through the lens of the contemporary culture, all the while making notes. The Spirit will quicken your intellect.

Confer with Flesh and Blood

After a thorough study of the context and the text, it is safe to "confer with flesh and blood" (Galatians 1:16, NKJV). I say "safe" because when the mind has been "programmed" by the Spirit, the comments of people will not drive the message, only enhance and enrich the truth. Men and women in the past put their best thinking into books and commentaries. The preacher who has access to a great library in hard copy or software is privileged. Let the Spirit impress your thinking as you read others. Do not bother to use anything that is not hard-hitting or does not excite you. This is key! If you are not influenced by something you read, it will not do much for the congregation if you repeat it.

The Lord uses all kinds of circumstances and experiences in the process of sermon building. Things that happened years ago will suddenly surface. Current events, an article in a magazine, or an incident at home will suddenly be relevant to the developing message.

Creating the Outline

The outline should be viewed as a track on which the message will run its course. In every sense of the word, it is a chain of logic, taking the hearer from the known to the unknown.

Before you is a mass of raw material, a wealth of truth—but it is all disconnected. The preacher's task is to surface the single great life-changing truth in the text and use the material gleaned to lead the hearer step-by-step into a prophetic moment of decision, a moment of powerful truth, so faith will stand upon the power of God, not human wisdom, and change a life. The overpowering truth may be a new insight into the grace of God, a call to repentance, a deposit of faith, a prophetic truth, a solemn warning, or a doctrinal statement. I have heard sermons built around "Help, Lord," "Knowing Is Not Enough; Living the Life Is What Counts," and "It Came to Pass, Not to Stay."

Ministers have the privilege of knowing before anyone else what the Spirit is saying to the church. The mind and soul are ablaze with divine truth. They have received the message for the hour. However, they are ahead of the congregation. God has spoken into their souls. Now they must speak God's Word in such a way as to lead others into that truth.

A cautionary statement of educators is "The limitation of the pupil is the limitation of the teacher." Jesus was aware of the principle. He was careful not to give His followers truth they could not conceptualize. The writer to the Hebrews spoke of milk for infants and solid food for the mature (Hebrews 5:13-14). Jesus was a master teacher because He skillfully took people from what they knew to what He wanted them to know.

The root meaning of communication is that which is common. It is the art of establishing and maintaining that which is common with another; hence, the parables of Jesus to introduce profound truth. The task of the preacher is to use the common in such a way as not lose the listener in reaching the ultimate goal of his message. This brings us back to the chain of logic—the effective outline.

See the Scope of the Subject

Amassing material without regard to logical progression allows the preacher to see the full scope of the subject. Otherwise, there is a tendency to treat a subject superficially instead of contextually. Out of all the compiled statements, words, and unfinished thoughts, the preacher will quickly discover recurring themes and emphases. They should be noted in some way as a means of beginning to prioritize what will ultimately be preached.

With overshadowing emphases in mind, the preacher should be able to decide the first link in the chain of logic from the gathered material. (This is different from the introduction, which we will address later.) The purpose of the first link, or major point, is to get the congregation on the same track.

Much has been written about the changes over the years in how people assimilate communication. Because of television and other high-tech tools, many psychologists believe circular learning has overtaken linear logic. For example, many programs are a series of events and subplots often isolated from a theme. The viewer learns through impressions more than logic. To some extent, this shift has affected how people listen and learn. It is the reason role playing, skits, and drama have become common in more churches. The visual has more impact than the auditory. However, systematic preaching has been ordained by God as the primary method to dispense truth. That is the reason why a Spirit-empowered message from the lips of an anointed preacher will always be relevant to any age in any culture.

On the Day of Pentecost, Peter started his chain of logic with the obvious. Something wonderful had happened. He said, "This is what was spoken by the prophet Joel" (Acts 2:16). Most of his congregation knew the prophecies. All of them had just observed the unusual phenomenon we call "glossolalia." Peter used this common event that interested everyone to lead to the culminating revelation of Jesus Christ as the risen Savior.

The chain of logic is a means to bring truth into alignment for the purpose of leveraging impact upon the mind. In every subject taught in schools and universities, the teacher regularly points to or reminds students of the familiar as a basis to teach the unknown.

The Middle of the Message

The middle of the message is where the "cause" is made for the final point. In most messages, it is the bridge that spans yesterday and tomorrow or the revelation of cause and effect. Peter's sermon at Pentecost is a dramatic illustration. The bulk of his sermon is taken up with the cause behind the effect of what the people saw. "You see the manifestation [speaking in tongues]. Now I'll tell you the reasons behind it [Jesus Christ crucified and risen again] so you can come to God in a way you have never known ["Repent and be baptized, every one of you"]" (Acts 2:14-41).

Paul's sermon to the Athenians in Acts 17 is a good example of a chain of logic:

Link 1: "I . . . found an altar with this inscription" (v.23).

Link 2: "Therefore since we are God's offspring, we should not think that the divine being is like gold or silver or stone—an image made by man's design and skill" (v.29).

Link 3: "For he has set a day when he will judge the world with justice by the man he has appointed. He has given proof of this to all men by raising him from the dead" (v.31).

In every case, the preacher is carrying a message of truth suffused in faith and hope. The goal is the announcement of God's power to transform lives and modify behavior to more clearly reflect Christ in the believer.

Filling in the Outline

After having established the chain of logic and major points, the preacher is ready to "put the meat on the bones" of the outline. This is done using the same process that established the chain of logic for the entire message. Under each major point, the preacher should develop a well-thought-out chain of logic with three or four powerful points. The mass of material originally gathered should prove to be a rich resource. Because the preacher knows the major truths and the path of the message, the brain will act like a magnet pulling out the important ideas and statements from among those first noted in order to strengthen and enrich the sermon. Throughout the process, the preacher will hear himself saying, "This statement must be used under point 2," or "This thought will strengthen point 3," etc.

Ready the Manuscript

After the outline is complete, the minister is ready to go to work on the manuscript, beginning with the introduction. A good introduction is the attention getter that should make the listener want to hear more. The introduction is different from the first link in the chain of logic, which is the initial step into the process of truth. Among other things, the introduction should communicate the preacher's interest in or concern for the listener, never the other way around. For example, Paul's introduction at Mars Hill contains both a compliment and an observation that his listeners are likely to accept: "Men of Athens! I see that in every way you are very religious" (Acts 17:22). Note that Peter, on the day of Pentecost, takes advantage of the crowd's curiosity: "Let me explain this to you" (Acts 2:14). And then some see a touch of humor in his refutation of the "tabloid" explanation going around: "These men are not drunk, as you suppose. It's only nine in the morning!" (Acts 2:15)

Furthermore, the introduction should communicate that what is coming is very important. In other words, the preacher is building a case for the message. It is like the statement on the dust cover of a book that emphasizes how important it is to buy the book. A psychologist might say the introduction is important because it affirms your listeners in the sense that from the beginning, they have chosen to spend their time wisely by listening to the preacher.

Not to Be Memorized

The manuscript need not be either memorized for preaching or read word for word. It is for the purpose of making certain that the thoughts have been crafted well enough to communicate the major points of the message. It forces the preacher to clearly articulate difficult concepts. When one writes out the message, one cannot cheat, meaning that the preacher cannot in good faith write down, "I'll say something about that when I preach this." I have heard of preachers who insert notes to themselves to "gesture here" or "shout hallelujah" there in their manuscripts. However, I feel that destroys spontaneity and goes beyond the purpose of a manuscript.

To Illustrate

The subject of illustrations cannot be overestimated. Very simply, they illustrate, or picture, the concept of truth in such a way the listener can "see" the truth, not just hear it. They bring the abstract into the concrete. An apt illustration can bring new awareness to an old truth.

A good preacher will be a good storyteller, Jesus himself offering no better example. To develop the art of illustrating the truth, it is necessary to learn the subtle nuances, progression, and pertinent facts that make the story or illustration most effective. It is not uncommon to hear people forget the punch line of a good story. Such an embarrassment can happen in the pulpit, especially with humor. Writing out illustrations in the manuscript usually results in avoiding this hazard.

A helpful technique in writing the manuscript is for the preacher to write as if he were a listener in the pew. (For many years, I have visualized a very cynical person sitting across my desk saying, "What difference does that statement make?") Too often, even the best preachers can fall into the trap of saying something because it sounds good but does not mean anything to the listener or add any value to the message.

To Preserve

One of the greatest reasons for writing the message is preservation. Effective messages are worth repeating in various settings when the Spirit quickens the truth afresh. The key is maintaining the freshness of the message. R. A. McClure was a great Pentecostal preacher. When asked if he preached the same sermon on occasion, he said, "Yes, I do. But before I preach it again, I lay it on the desk, point my finger at it, and say, 'Ye must be born again.'"

If preachers will write out their messages, they will save themselves a great deal of frustration and research time when it comes to preaching a message for the second time. Preserving just an outline is inadequate; in just a few days, the memory of particular points and illustrations fade. When the minister comes to the illustration and the outline says something like "The miracle in Brazil," he may need a miracle to recall it.

Come Back Another Day

Now the manuscript is finished. Putting it away is helpful. Coming back to it in a day or so generates a fresh perspective, "new eyes," allowing you to enrich the message further. Sometimes this exercise proves to be a bit discouraging. What excited the preacher yesterday may be flat today. Almost without exception, however, when the minister begins to pray for new insights and divine help, the message comes alive again with even more power. In extreme cases, the preacher may feel what was prepared has gone so flat he must start over with a totally different sermon. God will honor that kind of integrity and give the preacher great liberty.

The enriching process is not for changing the goal of the message; it is for achieving greater inspiration, clarity, and application. If the message survives the writing and enriching process, it is not only ready to be proclaimed but also ready to be proclaimed with a strong sense of authority.

There is nothing in the world like the thrill experienced by a Pentecostal preacher who is well-prepared both spiritually and mentally. He knows he has a message of redemption and healing for the godless, the brokenhearted, and the fearful.

Simply Report

When the message is delivered, let the preacher be at his personal best, knowing he has not created the good news but is simply reporting it. Let him allow the Spirit to flow in power and conviction.

The Altar Call

The message is delivered. Hopefully, it was good news. Now let the people respond to the call of the altar. In my experience, those who are not moved enough spiritually to move physically seldom change. The pride or fear that holds them back publicly will not be broken privately. Sometime, somewhere, they must declare unashamedly their need for faith in God. The most opportune time is when the Spirit of God is moving in their heart and soul.

The Pentecostal altar is more than a symbol. It is a focal point of faith, a point of contact between a person and God, the place where the Spirit's power begins the process of transformation. For Spirit-filled preachers, for those whose eye of faith is on the altar, it is the capstone, the supreme reward for the many hours of prayer and study. A well-prepared, Spirit-filled pulpit will beget a well-filled, Spirit-convicting altar, an altar of repentant sinners and hungry believers. May we as America's Pentecostal preachers do our part.

God has certainly done all that is necessary to make the gospel we preach in His name "the power of God for the salvation of everyone who believes" (Romans 1:16).

Let every Pentecostal preacher respond by making a covenant with God to do everything he can to justify God's ordination and anointing upon his life and ministry.